EFFECTIVE
PR
MANAGEMENT

EFFECTIVE
PR
MANAGEMENT

A Guide to Corporate Success

PAUL WINNER

Kogan
Page

To my wife Mary, and to
Sonya and Daniel

First published in 1987 by
Kogan Page Ltd,
120 Pentonville Rd, London N1 9JN

Revised edition 1990

Typeset by CG Graphic Services, Tring, Herts
Printed and bound in Great Britain by
Biddles Ltd, Guildford and King's Lynn

British Library Cataloguing in Publication Data
Winner, Paul
   Effective PR management – Rev. ed.
   1. Public relations
   I. Title
   659.2

ISBN 0-7494-0070-6

Contents

Preface

It is today widely recognised that public relations has a crucial role to play in the total business system. The survival and effectiveness of any organisation are now seen to depend on the relationships it establishes with its 'publics'.

Understanding and managing the complexity of relationships which exist between today's increasingly open organisations is the basic function of public relations. While few would dispute this fact, not everybody is convinced of the ability of PR practitioners to perform this fundamental role.

It is the aim of this book to demonstrate the central role which the PR department or agency can and should play in the running of an efficient organisation, and to show how public relations is becoming an intrinsic part of every other management function.

Effective public relations depends in many ways on achieving the right balance: the balance between formality and flexibility in organisation structure; between encouraging innovation and relying on experience and precedent; between over-reacting and under-reacting to events. This book considers the choices to be made; it evaluates the relevance to PR of current management techniques and suggests appropriate ways of using the many good ideas contained in the literature of management theory. It also presents some original techniques for improving PR management.

Extensive interviews with decision-makers in the PR departments of a number of nationalised industries, large private corporations, local authorities and external agencies were an important part of the research for this book, and their views, which are quoted throughout the text provide a very valuable insight into various aspects in the practice of public relations.

My own experience in building one of the top 15 independent consultancies between 1967 and 1984 and then selling it in 1984 to the largest and first fully listed, publicly quoted PR company, has highlighted what is still the weakest element in the PR industry, namely the management function.

The book should appeal to practitioners at various levels within PR organisations and to those wishing to enter the industry; it has been written with the requirements of the CAM syllabus in mind. It should also be of interest to those paying for the services of the PR practitioner and to those concerned with PR as part of the general management of an organisation.

Paul Winner
October 1989

Acknowledgements

This book would not have been possible without the help of Penelope Silver whose contribution to the structure and research was invaluable.

I would like to thank CAM, the Communication Advertising and Marketing Education Foundation Ltd, the IPR (Institute of Public Relations), and the PRCA (Public Relations Consultants Association) for their assistance.

Special thanks are due to Irene Miller, my PA for 18 years, who participated in the growth and development of Paul Winner Marketing Communications Ltd and who has assisted me in the growth of my new company, Paul Winner Consultants Ltd, established in June 1986; to Marion Neal, whose contribution to effective financial management has been invaluable; and also to Donald Mackay for his meticulous attention to detail in proof reading the text of this book and eliminating most of the jargon.

I wish to thank my wife Mary and my children, Sonya and Daniel, for their patience during the agonising moments in the writing of this book.

Finally, I am indebted to the organisations and practitioners whose comments are quoted in this book.

Chapter 1

The Role of PR in the Total Business System

The central argument of this book is that public relations can and should play a many-sided role in organisational life. But the potential scope of public relations extends beyond the traditional functions of press relations, financial, corporate, industrial and technical communications. This has yet to be fully recognised. Increasingly the public relations practitioner is now involved in strategic planning, government and industrial relations. The argument here is that it is proper and practical, as well as strategically sound, for the public relations function within an organisation to include the broad strategic positioning of an organisation within its total environment. Social responsibility, community relations, communication with all levels of government both within the United Kingdom and in international markets, particularly the EEC, are all areas relevant to the public relations practitioner.

However real progress in this direction cannot be made until a reasonable working definition of public relations is established, covering its objectives and scope of operation. The confusing and even contradictory ideas which have existed up to now make it very difficult for public relations people to practise effectively.

The following discussion of the problem of defining the public relations role is included not purely for its academic interest but in the hope that it will shed light on the best way forward.

WHAT IS PR?

The literature offers numerous definitions of public relations;

indeed it seems that everyone who has had even a passing flirtation with public relations has been anxious to come up with the magic formula. But it is almost impossible to find two definitions which share common ground, and their value in practice is negligible.

The Institute of Public Relations defines PR as 'the deliberate, planned and sustained effort to establish mutual understanding between the organisation and its publics'. It has been described as 'the engineering of consent', which presents us with an interesting concept but is not sufficiently specific to be practical. According to *Fortune* magazine, public relations is 'good performance, publicly appreciated because adequately communicated'. But this covers only one aspect of the public relations function; it ignores the role of public relations in explaining the reasons for poor performance, and of course it excludes from consideration a wide range of situations which have nothing to do with performance as such, whether good, bad or indifferent. Public relations has elsewhere been described as 'the management function which gives the same organised and careful attention to the aspect of goodwill as it gives to any other major asset of the business'. But this definition assumes a closed system model of the organisation, and does not consider the role of public relations between organisations – which is increasingly important. More ambitious is the view that public relations 'is a combination of philosophy, sociology, economics, language, psychology, journalism and communication in a system of human understanding'. This may be true, but it does not provide the public relations practitioner with a very useful brief.

A common definition is so elusive because public relations is having to contend with important moral and ethical issues, as well as practical ones, on which opinions and attitudes vary enormously. At the moment these are dealt with on an ad hoc basis, but practitioners need to develop an intelligent appreciation of these issues and a coherent method of dealing with the problems which arise.

The relationship between public relations and the press raises many fundamental questions. It is very difficult to draw a distinction between objective editorial comment and public relations input, and between public relations and direct advertising. Opinions differ widely on what is or what should be the impact of public relations on 'factual' press reporting. One nationalised industry's PR director contrasted his own views with those of some of his colleagues:

> They would sometimes have different opinions about the role of the public press, and some very senior people think that the press ought to be helping industry to solve its problems and helping Britain. But I do not think that is what the newspapers are there for. The danger of that type of thing would be that you would be working towards a managed system of news such as they have in the Soviet Union, which I think is totally unhealthy and anti-democratic, and would demand misgiving. I think the press could spend more time talking about achievements and progress, but I do not think that is really a moral obligation. They exist to sell newspapers. I should like to see a more even balance of political opinions in the national press, but I can only live with the situation as it exists, and I cannot dictate the political attitudes of the Daily Express and the Daily Mail. . . .

The Institute of Journalists' conference in 1980 was warned that:

> Journalists are increasingly misinformed by the government and others who attempt to manipulate the news. The Institute's President also said that journalists are being asked more often to suppress news because 'it would be in the public interest' to do so.

The role which public relations plays in organisational life, and particularly the importance attached to it in relation to other management activities, varies considerably. It can, for instance, vary between industries; PR in the financial community is seen by some as different from PR in the industrial field.

> It became ever more clear to me that PR as it applies to a bank or insurance company is very different from PR in industry or as it applies to a company producing a product which is going to be marketed and sold.

This view is common to the specialists in different fields even though the basic function remains similar. The execution of the PR role also varies greatly, and, for instance, in the financial sector, evaluating its effectiveness is problematic because of the intangible factors involved.

The range of variation and the factors which cause it are examined in the case studies presented in later chapters. But there are points of agreement which emerge from the research interviews:

> I do not see PR as being a modern term that I would want to use at all quite frankly. I find that it nowhere near covers the sort of activities that I am responsible for. I consider my job to be improving the empathy between management and a large number of 'publics'.

The public relations director of one nationalised industry, who is responsible for the board's external and internal information services and publicity throughout the country through press and broadcasting, advertising and lectures, estimates that at least half of his department's effort is directed at communications within the industry. This effort includes, for instance, generating a feeling of identity across the industry, and smoothing relocation problems. In terms of external relationships, he thinks that the real importance of PR

> . . . comes almost in a negative way. We have a tremendous potential for damaging the industry. In the case of a press officer, perhaps, taking a telephone call at home late at night, which they do, and perhaps giving a careless answer to a reporter . . . he could cause a strike . . . which would lose us thousands of pounds' worth of business.

Inaction can have as far reaching and damaging an effect as careless action.

> There is always a very strong school of thought about that, especially in the insurance industry, that tends to be a bit, maybe, introspective, and prefers to get on with its business and not be involved in this difficult thing of PR. People would like to be able to say 'Don't do anything, just adopt a low profile.' But we cannot do that all the time. We are too big, too important, have too many other influences on other people to adopt such a low profile. . . . The only result of doing that is that questions are unanswered in people's minds as to what we are really up to. But other people who are interested in us are going to make statements about us, so we have to do something about that. But there is always, I find, a fair body of opinion which says 'Well, perhaps you're right, maybe we'll leave it this time round, tomorrow morning it'll go away . . . people will forget about it.' But in the meantime somebody's opinion may have been changed about what you are.

The target audience for public relations is determined by the activities of the organisation and any current problem areas. Public relations is often concerned with reaching what are loosely called the opinion formers, that is the press, MPs, government officials and consumer groups. But in each specific situation the target audience will also comprise those groups in the environment with which the organisation deals; these are now increasingly described in the literature as the organisation's 'publics'. It is a simple matter to identify the relevant groups for any given organisation.

A PRACTICAL DEFINITION OF PR

It is sufficient to say that PR is concerned with maintaining harmonious and understanding relationships between all the various parts of an organisation and all the groups which have a relationship with it. This could mean management, workers, shareholders, trade unions, suppliers, customers and government.

This definition of PR derives directly from developments in the area of organisation theory. Conflicting interests or competing goals exist within every organisation; eg workers' pursuance of their own best interests may be counter-productive and hence disruptive to those of management and the organisation overall. An open systems view of organisation recognises that there are many separate groups both within the organisation and outside it, all of which have vested interests. To a large degree it is the organisation's ability to cope with the inevitable conflicts of interest which determines its effectiveness. The role of public relations is to try to resolve, or at least minimise, conflict through persuasion and influence; to avoid the need for forceful intervention such as strike action by a trade union or new legislation by government.

> I see it as a straightforward process of communication, of making people understand accurately and effectively the things that you want to make them understand, that you feel they should understand so that they are able to make decisions and reactions which in turn impinge upon whatever you want to do.

This is a very different kind of process from advertising, where one is concerned, not with maintaining a delicate balance between different groups, but with the simpler process of persuading one clearly defined group of people to behave in a particular way.

PR AND OTHER AREAS OF MANAGEMENT

The relationship between public relations and other management processes depends to a large extent on the particular organisation. In a sales-oriented company public relations is often allied to marketing and selling. News releases may really be a back up to advertising in trade and technical journals; effectiveness can be evaluated in terms of numbers of reader enquiries. When one is dealing with intangibles, with ideas, the link between public relations and marketing is less apparent and less easy to evaluate.

A lot of people today I understand are trying to marry marketing and PR, so the PR will be measured against the effectiveness of the marketing programme. So if, for example, a company will take various target audiences or target accounts and the PR

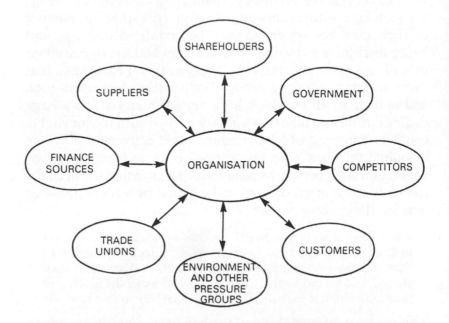

Figure 1
The environment of a manufacturing organisation

department will use its techniques to establish a greater understanding and knowledge of the product, then it is now possible through that application of PR to give a bottom-line figure to it, if you like. In banking, that is not possible.

It is arguable that even in banking and insurance a bottom-line evaluation should be attempted!

There is one critical distinction between public relations and the allied functions of marketing, advertising and selling. Public relations essentially provides a service, not only to the organisation but also to individual departments on a needs basis.

> I suppose the one thing which is different about public affairs from marketing is that however hard one works there are not all that number of areas where you make the final decision. There seem to be an awful lot of things where you are advising people to do things.

It may be a reflection of this weakness in the function of public relations that very often inadequate resources are deployed for getting information; staffing is often inadequate with no provision for extra (buffer) facilities to deal with unanticipated situations. Although increasingly recognised as playing a critical role, the public relations function is typically under-financed. Many organisations spend millions of pounds on advertising, and below-the-line commercial activity, but very little on public relations. Taking all the organisations in the UK, not more than 10 per cent of their total advertising fund is spent on public relations. In terms of manpower, a very small percentage of time is spent on the PR function. For instance: a personnel director is often highly skilled in the personnel function – selection, analysis of qualities, salary reviews etc – but tends to have had very little training in communications.

But this situation seems likely to improve in the next few years as a consequence of two facts: public relations is broadening its scope, and it is also becoming recognised as an increasingly critical function.

> I think it has changed a lot already, noticeably, in recent years, and I suspect it is probably going to change more. Again, change is often generated by what is going on outside.

During the 1960s, marketing was very much in vogue. Many marketing men rose through the ranks to head up their organisations. It is impossible to say whether having marketing men in key positions helped generate a climate sympathetic to the marketing concept, or whether, conversely, marketing was seen to be the newest panacea for all organisational ills (exponential growth was the solution to all problems) so that key posts were offered to marketing men. A similar process was observable when financial problems then became paramount and finance men moved in to head up large organisations.

	Category of Processual Relationship	Unit of Analysis	Level of Analysis
	processess internal to the organisation	individual group	micro-level
Organisation	processes which cross the organisational boundary	organisation	macro-level
Environment	processes external to the organisation	interorgan-isation	

Figure 2
The three basic categories of processual relationship

The vogue problem today is communications. But while there is a surprisingly high degree of consensus about the definition of the problem, the question remains whether or not public relations practitioners can and should assume the responsibility. Many ex-marketing men have gone in to head up public affairs functions. Is this because similar personality types are attracted to both public relations/public affairs and marketing, or is it a question of being sympathetic to future market trends?

The (good) public relations man is becoming accepted as the business confidante of many Chief Executives and Board Chairmen; this is the traditional management consultant's role but the current trend is probably sensible. The PR relationship is essentially empathetic, interpretive and continuous, whereas the management consultant tends to impose and work to completed task patterns. Public relations agencies are providing market intelligence. Some perform a wholesaling function of bringing together and directing an ad hoc project team for specific assignments.

There has been a very significant attempt recently to marry public relations with marketing. The argument has been between the purist and the generalist. The North American public relations scene, which the British have tended to follow, has moved on from the generalist approach, and seems to be reverting to a purist public relations stance. But there seem to be sound theoretical reasons why the generalist approach should be preferred here. The PR marketing man who generalises has a better grasp of the corporate nature of his organisation; with broader perspectives he can make a more significant contribution.

It is increasingly important for organisations to function as openly as possible. Obtaining and accurately interpreting information about changes in the environment clearly necessitates effective two-way communication between the organisation and the external groups with which it deals. There must also be some control of the communication between those various groups, so that conflict is minimised. This is the role of public relations . . . or could be.

ORGANISATION SUPPORT

The effectiveness of public relations depends on a variety of factors which are examined in Chapter 2. However, in organisation terms, the support given to the function by the chief executive is critical, particularly in the early stages before the personal credibility of the PR man has been established. Without the right man at the top, the most sophisticated function within the organisation is likely to be stunted. Another factor often critical to the success of the PR effort is whether or not the public relations head is on the board and hence privy to all confidential information.

We are lucky here because the Board do give it high standing. I go to all the Board Meetings, I am directly responsible to the

Chairman. So we are not so much used as a fire service when something has gone wrong. If difficult things are coming up, most people . . . all levels of management . . . will remember to tip off the PRO. It is worth far more than if the man is taken by surprise.

I attend all the Board Meetings. My predecessor's predecessor did not attend any of these meetings. The Chairman has been the instigator of this, and he has made it abundantly clear that he considers communications to be a vitally important task, and I cannot communicate and I cannot give the kind of service that he wants, unless I know exactly what is going on.

And if the senior PR man is not involved at the senior executive level then probably the decision has been made that they wanted a dog to do the dog's job rather than to do a proper PR job.

Chapter 2

Organisation Structure

FORMALISATION/FLEXIBILITY

The key to all aspects of organisation structure can be seen to be the extent to which roles are specified, and, on the other hand, the range of legitimate discretion which the organisation allows the individual. The problem is how to fix the ratio between *formalisation* and *flexibility*.

In an organisation where roles are highly specified, where there is a high degree of formalisation, there is inevitably little flexibility, little opportunity for individual discretion. Conversely, where roles are relatively unstructured, and there is a low degree of formalisation, there is much more scope for individuals to use discretion, and consequently the organisation is much more flexible.

If we elaborate this distinction between formalisation and flexibility we can list a number of characteristics of each kind of organisation structure:

Highly structured roles	Unstructured
Limited discretion	High discretion
Inflexible	Flexible
Formalised	Informal
Easily disciplined	Hard to discipline

Hierarchy	v	Participation
Standardisation	v	Personal contribution
Specialisation	v	Common goals (generalist)
Equality	v	Recognition of merit

In public relations organisations (whether internal operations

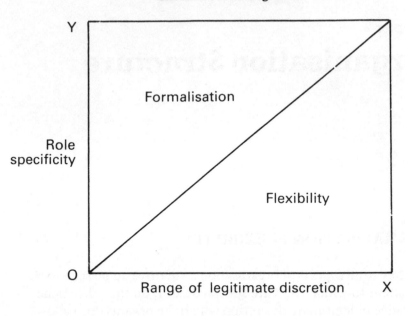

Figure 3
Organisation structure: formalisation/flexibility

or external agencies, and in similar organisations such as design consultancies and advertising agencies, it is crucial to identify and maintain the right balance between individual creativity and organisation responsibility; innovation and consistency in performance; inventiveness and cost effectiveness; autonomy and clearly defined roles.

DIMENSIONS OF ORGANISATION STRUCTURE

Organisation structure can be looked at in terms of the following three dimensions:

1. *Structuring of activities*
    The degree to which the behaviour of employees is defined, incorporating the degree of role specialisation in task allocation, the degree of standardisation of organisation routines, and the degree of formalisation of written procedures.

22

2. *Concentration of authority*
    The degree to which authority for decisions rests in controlling units outside the organisation and is central-ised at the higher hierarchical levels within it.

3. *Line control of workflow*
    The degree to which self control is exercised by line personnel as against its exercise through impersonal procedures.

Looking again at the opposing characteristics of organisation structure listed above, any organisation which tends toward the lefthand side (ie is hierarchical, standardised, specialised and egalitarian) is described as a bureaucracy. Bureaucratic forms of organisation are also described in the literature of organisa-tion theory as 'mechanistic'; non-bureaucratic organisations, in contrast, are described as organismic.

Mechanistic management system

This is characterised by:

1. The *specialised differentiation* of functional tasks into which the problems and tasks facing the concern as a whole are broken down.

2. The *abstract nature* of each individual task, which is pursued with techniques and purposes more or less distinct from those of the concern as a whole.

3. The reconciliation, for each level in the hierarchy, of these distinct performances by the *immediate superiors*.

4. The *precise definition* of rights and obligations and technical methods attached to each functional role.

5. The *translation of rights and obligations* and methods into the responsibilities of a functional position.

6. *Hierarchic structure* of control, authority and com-munication.

7. A reinforcement of the hierarchic structure by the location of *knowledge* of actualities exclusively *at the top* of the hierarchy.

8. A tendency for *vertical interaction* between members, ie between superior and subordinate.

9. A tendency for operations and working behaviour to be *governed by superiors*.

10. *Insistence on loyalty* to the concern and obedience to superiors as a condition of membership.

11. A greater importance and prestige attaching to *internal* (local) than to general (cosmopolitan) knowledge, experience and skill.

Organismic management system

This, in contrast, is characterised by:

1. The *contributive nature* of special knowledge and experience to the common task of the concern.

2. The *realistic* nature of the individual task, which is seen as set by the total situation of the concern.

3. The adjustment and *continual redefinition* of individual tasks through interaction with others.

4. The *shedding of responsibility* as a limited field of rights, obligations and methods. (Problems may not be posted upwards, downwards or sideways.)

5. The *spread of commitment* to the concern beyond any technical definition.

6. A *network structure* of control, authority and communication.

7. Omniscience no longer imputed to the head of the concern; *knowledge* may be located anywhere in the network; this location becomes the centre of authority.

8. A *lateral* rather than a vertical direction of communication through the concern.

9. A content of communication which consists of *information and advice* rather than instructions and decisions.

10. *Commitment* to the concern's tasks and to the 'technological ethos' of material progress and expansion is more highly valued than loyalty.

11. Importance and prestige attach to *affiliations and expertise* valid in the industrial, technical and commercial milieux external to the firm.

A QUESTION OF BALANCE

It is now generally accepted that there is no such thing as the *best* organisation structure. One needs a balance between the two extremes of a *mechanistic* and an *organismic* organisation, but the correct balance for any given situation depends on a number of identifiable *contingencies*. That is to say, different organisation structures are best suited to different organisation tasks; the best organisation structure will depend upon the particular situation.

These factors derive from the formalisation/flexibility distinction illustrated in Figure 3 above.

1. *Size*

    Overall size has been shown in several surveys to be closely associated with type of organisation structure, especially in the size range 100–5000 employees. Organisation growth is associated with increasing complexity: the number of levels of management increases; problems of delegation and control increase; the number of separate specialist groups grows, so increasing the problems of coordination.

2. *Diversification*

    Diversification usually brings about a modification in organisation structure, typically through some form of divisionalisation.

3. *Environment*

    Environment conditions have important implications for the type of organisation structure which is the most effective. The key issue is the stability of the environment – how much uncertainty the organisation is facing.

    ITT provides an example: when faced with a climate of chronic uncertainty about the future of its telephone business in countries such as Chile, it built up a highly developed system of political intelligence to provide the necessary anticipatory and adaptive capacity.

4. *Technology*

    Technology is now seen more as a constraining than a determining factor in organisation structure. For example, any effect the introduction of computers may have on centralisation is probably due more to management's philosophy on centralising information and control than to the presence of the computer technology per se.

5. *Personnel*
The personnel in the organisation will affect the organisation structure, eg large numbers of staff specialists.

Three points should be borne in mind when considering these structural factors:

(a) Achievement of the organisation's objectives will be more likely if it adopts realistic policies, and its structure is designed to satisfy these policies. To illustrate: when a small sweets manufacturer decided to expand out of its traditional high quality market to produce a low price line for a chainstore, production could not be maintained at the new higher rate necessary for this contract because the company was still operating its previous (stringent) quality control policies.

(b) Factors of environment, size, technology and personnel vary between departments and divisions within an organisation.

(c) Structural factors are themselves interrelated, eg larger companies are generally the more diversified.

STRATEGIES FOR CONTROL

In a bureaucratic organisation, decision making authority is decentralised down to the holders of official roles. These are structured to take account of their specialised prescribed duties. A system of procedure and documentation is designed to limit areas of discretion, as well as to provide information on role performance.

Formalised procedures impose restraints. This encourages the development of a less centralised authority structure, and this in turn facilitates more flexible decision taking. So, as organisations regulate more and more behaviours, they decentralise. The reverse is also true: when organisations rely less on standard procedures for regulating and recording behaviour, other things being equal, they tend to centralise decision taking.

This gives two strategies for control:

(a) maintaining control directly by keeping decisions at high levels (hierarchic); or

(b) maintaining control indirectly by relying on procedures.

In a bureaucratic situation, both of these strategies of control may be used to try to achieve coordination between various groups of specialists with different goals. But both have their problems. With the direct use of *hierarchical control*, the higher up the decision is taken, the further away it is from the problem, and the greater the divergence between what was decided and what actually happens. With *control by procedure*, the danger is that the correct carrying out of systems may become more important than the coordination and control they were designed to facilitate, and, worse, it may have a negative effect. For instance, it is generally accepted that too rigid adherence to budgets or purchasing procedures may reduce an organisation's capacity to adapt to change quickly enough.

Problems of bureaucracy

Three points need to be made here. First, several writers have suggested important negative consequences of bureaucratic organisation – although they have not disputed the contention that it is the most *efficient* form of organisation in terms of achieving the goals of the formal hierarchy. These consequences include:

- reduction in the number of personal relationships
- rigidity in the implementation of organisation rules
- increased use of categorisation as a decision making technique which decreases the search for alternatives (rigid behaviour)
- increased difficulty with clients of organisation
- increased use of trappings of authority
- by defining unacceptable behaviour, rules also define the minimum acceptable behaviour.

Second, problems develop where instead of *adapting* a

bureaucratic structure, the system is just reinforced. For instance, by the setting up of committees overlaying the existing bureaucracy; the creation of 'super persons'; the creation of additional branches of the hierarchy; the creation of intermediaries. 'Nonpersons unperson persons.'

Third, all organisations have the weaknesses of their strengths; and the corollary of this is that all organisations have the strengths of their weaknesses, *if* they are prepared to accept those weaknessses. Strengths build into the weaknesses. If you ask an organisation what are its strengths, those are its weaknesses. The weakness of bureaucracy is therefore precisely its success. The significance of an organisation's weaknesses will be determined by the particular situation. The task of adapting in bureaucratic organisations is particularly important in a turbulent and rapidly changing environment.

THE APPLICATION OF ORGANISATION STRUCTURE PRINCIPLES TO PR

Most PR organisations belong to the organismic type because of the nature of their activity. The fact that growth tends to produce an increasing degree of bureaucracy explains why so many public relations operations remain relatively small.

The relationship between structure and process is a problem which continues to provoke much academic debate; this is fuelled by the difficulty of establishing any tests of the concepts involved. Organisation structure either facilitates or impedes organisation processes.

The problems of finding the best structure are common to all types of organisation, though the balance and the range of solutions varies between different situations and sets of circumstances; the best structure is determined by a number of sometimes unrelated factors. Public relations organisations are particularly tricky in this respect because accurate evaluation of effective public relations is difficult. (The reasons for this and the range of possible solutions are explored later.) Where evaluation of the creative public relations input is a problem, so too is any attempt to define performance. And if performance cannot readily be defined, neither can it be easily controlled or monitored, and the whole process of planning becomes weakened.

From research, it has been possible to abstract generalisations about which kind of organisation structures seem to work most effectively in the public relations field. External public relations operations tend to be structured on the basis of client accounts, or grouping of client accounts; these are in effect the various groups in the environment with which the agency deals.

INTERNAL PR OPERATIONS

A typical structure divides into:

- Public relations office (Publicity)
- Press office
- Publications unit
- Film unit.

We have a Press Office which really comes under the operational side of the set-up. The Press Office deals with press releases, press enquiries and so on, and I think that works quite well because we have found that, over a period of time, we have been able to build up a relationship with the press, and therefore if something happens in the insurance industry we tend to get a telephone call from people in the press, to the chap in the Press Office whom they know, saying: 'What do you think about so and so?' or 'Can you give me any background?', or 'Would your company like to comment on this?' As a result I think we probably do get a bit more publicity than most other companies, actually.

There is a Press Office with about 10 people that deal with press enquiries and those press enquiries are in two categories. There is the selective and the enforced, and I try to get them to maintain a balance of selective and enforced. The enforced one is obviously where you pick up the telephone, answer a question, and the selective one is where you say 'Well, we are not getting over to this media and that media and so forth.'

Publications units vary from a department of three men (as compared with the press unit in the same government organisation of only two people) responsible for 'the great mass of print and publicity that comes out, and which is translated into booklets, brochures, leaflets, stickers . . .' to the Publications

Section of the Health and Safety Executive which 'is a key part of the structure. We have a bigger turnout of publications almost than any other government department.'

The publicity part of internal public relations operations seems to vary considerably both in resources allocated to it and scope of responsibility. Typically it deals with direct mail advertising, conferences and exhibitions, and it will cover visual displays, lecture inputs and demonstrations. The Health and Safety Executive operates its own internal film unit, and has produced about 21 films in total, all of those full-length films on either specific subjects and problems or broad health and safety philosophy. In contrast, the public relations head of an American bank uses outside support services.

> Because of our limited, very small staff, I use an outside advertising agency, printers, design people who will help me put together a presentation. And because of my years in Fleet Street I know the people up there who, if I do not have time to write a speech or an article I will call on a friendly journalist who will do something for me on a freelance basis. . . . So I can run what is a very complicated department with a variety of things because I have those outside services. They are not on contract, they are freelance people. . . . I use them occasionally because the requirement is so specialised that I could not do it without a lot of research, but also when it becomes impossible for me I cry out and I bring them in literally to assist me. But I do not use a full-time public relations consultancy. I do the work that they would do; I do that myself.

- Internal communications is a key part of the internal public relations operation's activities, and increasingly this is seen to be the case. In scope, this extends from the publications unit producing some kind of house journal, to an altogether more ambitious concept: 'We try to communicate with people in the terms which will be acceptable to them.'

> I suppose one of the most complicated areas, believe it or not, is dealing with our own staff. I believe that there is more misunderstanding between the management and its staff in a vast organisation – and I am not necessarily confining myself to my own industry here – than in almost any other field.

The following anecdote clearly illustrates the point. A bank manager in his late fifties said 'Goodnight' as usual to his staff on Friday night, dropping his assistant off at the station at seven o'clock. He died of a heart attack in the early hours of Saturday morning. First thing on Monday morning the senior person responsible told the assistant that he would put up a notice to inform the staff of the manager's death; the incredulous assistant could manage no response other than to say 'You do it your way, but allow me to do it mine.'

The basic activities are fairly standard over a range of different internal public relations operations, and the organisation structures developed to carry out those activities are similar. Any variation tends to be in overall size, and resources – both manpower and finance. The sample ranged from a full-time staff of nearly 200 in the public relations function of one government department, to 40 in one of the clearing banks, 20 in local government, and less than 10 in several medium to large organisations, in both the private and public sectors.

Size seems to depend more on management attitude – being 'public relations conscious' is the phrase frequently used – than on industrial sector or size of company in terms of assets: one of the clearing banks has a public relations facility employing more than 40 people, an American bank has less than 10, and a large insurance company has a public relations head who is also in fact company secretary. All similar organisations, of similar size in operating and capitalisation terms, all in the same sector, but with very different emphases on public relations.

For internal public relations operations, regardless of size, the main operating problems seem to be:

1. The range of different groups within the environment with which the public relations function must develop (satisfactory) relationships, and the problems of building these links in to the internal structure.

> Certainly in the financial public relations area we are talking about the groups that we have just mentioned, which is press, shareholders, stock market, investment analysts, and there is even a different range of audiences within the shareholders, of course, because you have institutional shareholders like us and you have Aunt Bertha and so on, and you have to think about them all. . . . This is one of the great difficulties about trying to do effective PR, because the target audience is a bit diffuse, and . . . I think that the great difficulty that we all have is trying to talk to Aunt Bertha, who does not

really understand very much about financial matters anyway, and how do you do that against the background where all the specialists are asking you for more and more information. It is not an easy one to resolve. . . . One of the things we try to do in our Annual Report to help a bit is to have a sort of simplified financial statement at the front and then the more technical stuff for those that know their way around these things a bit later. But it is not easy because I think that the target audience is a very wide one.

The conflicting needs of various 'user' groups are one of the major considerations in the design of any information system, whether internal or external.

2. In terms of responsibility for public relations, there seems to be a certain delicacy between line management and the public relations function. One can appreciate the problems. First, public relations is both a conscious activity and, of course, part of the way in which every individual in the organisation behaves both to other people within that organisation and to the world at large. Second, public relations is essentially an advisory function and not seen to be a significant part of the decision making process per se. Public relations considerations influence the choice between possible decisions (government subsidies to declining industries provide an obvious example). In this context, the importance of open support for the public relations function from the chief executive is obvious.

Some public relations heads feel a lack of support from other functions; sometimes this extends to a disagreement among colleagues about how to handle potentially difficult situations vis à vis the press. The public relations head of an American bank occasionally finds it difficult to convince senior line management that an open, honest approach to the press is the best policy.

Some senior officials in one of the nationalised industries take the view that the role of the press is to help industry to print comment that is favourable to management, and in this view they differ from the industry's public relations chief who believes that above all the press must be free.

The conflict is sometimes exacerbated by the geographical distances between head office and branches.

> Not only do we have people at the headquarters, but also we have, at our other levels of management within the organisation, like at the regional headquarters and indeed in a lower level at the divisional level, people who are public relations or public affairs experts, who get functional guidance from me and who are part of the management of the local organisation they are located in. For example, with the ever-expanding use of local radio, I will give them functional guidance as to how we should deal with this phenomenon, and these people will carry out that function within the framework of the general management within the area.

> There are always conflicts where you have a headquarters and regional levels underneath it, if you have within the regional levels financial accountability and general management control, because it means that functionally I cannot order the public relations people to do things, I have to advise and cajole and persuade them to do things. And in a way it slows up the process of management. But on the other hand, if I had immediate control over these people and could tell them to do things which they must do, then I could affect the financial structure of the region.

3. A basic problem in organising public relations is that its scope covers both on-going, continuous work and also ad hoc tasks. These are like a series of continuous eruptions on the surface of the existing workload. 'Eruptions' rather than 'interruptions' – the term which management generally uses advisedly, since the public relations team cannot afford to be continually interrupted. So while the on-going tasks can to a certain extent be planned and controlled, there must be planning of a kind to cope with such contingencies.

   One solution is to bring in extra resources from outside on a temporary basis, as a kind of buffer. Another way to match the resources to the needs is to redeploy existing staff. For example, to co-opt people to help with ad hoc projects like exhibitions at a local level.

Here the problem becomes one of delegation, and the perennial question is whether one delegates work or responsibility.

Finally, there are some very interesting developments in the role of public relations noted from the views which public relations chiefs hold about the growth and changes in their own operations. Most seem sure that a significant change comes from some kind of external impetus: a changed corporate objective in the case of NEDO, a general conditioning of society to expect higher standards of safety in the case of the Health and Safety Executive.

EXTERNAL PUBLIC RELATIONS AGENCIES

The key problem for the organisation structure of external public relations agencies is to cope with on-going workloads and ad hoc tasks at the same time. The option available to internal operations of going outside is hardly so attractive to a competitive agency, and so the flexibility must be in-built. This is largely a question of 'role structuring' and maintaining good working relationships between the various parts of the organisation. This range of possibilities of organisation design is discussed next.

Chapter 3

Role Problems: Conflict, Ambiguity and Stress

Organisations are no more and no less than composites of individual human personalities.

If all behaviour were totally random and completely unpredictable any kind of social existence ('social' here means interacting with other people) would be extremely difficult if not intolerable for most of us. Fortunately, human behaviour does tend to exhibit certain standard patterns. Within any organisation, people occupying particular positions will be expected to behave in particular ways. Frequently positions carry clearly visible labels: eg mode of dress, style of office, calibre of car. Such labels provide clues to any individual's position within the organisation, and so help other people to select appropriate ways of behaving towards them. Consequently, each position becomes associated with a defined range of acceptable behaviours and these act to a greater or lesser degree as a constraint on the natural behaviour of the individual.

Considerable problems can emerge, both for the individual and the organisation as a whole, where there exists either conflict or ambiguity about the range of expected behaviours. The identification of such problems, and their resolution, is discussed below.

THE CONCEPT OF ROLE

Social systems – whether organisations, work groups or the family – are made up of a set of related social positions. Associated with every position in an organisation is a set of activities and expected ways of behaving. These form the basis of the *role* to be performed for that position. A role is a set of expectations applied to the occupant of a position. In this way the concept of role links the individual personality into the organisation.

Associated with any given role is a set of expected behaviours. This expected standard of behaviour is essential in any social system, to introduce a certain level of certainty and stability into human relationships. An important part of the socialisation process involves developing an understanding of the responses of other individuals, so that these responses may be predicted and behaviour modified accordingly. If there were no stability or certainty about people's behaviour patterns, there could be no social interaction and hence no organisations. It is precisely because of the regularity of behaviour associated with specific roles that organisations and societies exist over and above the sum of the individuals within them.

A role can be visualised as the *context within which behaviour takes place*. This context is defined by the *structure and environment of the organisation*. But within the defined role, the behaviour of the role occupant will also be affected by many *variables*, eg his own personality, his response to other individuals, and indeed their response to his behaviour.

The crucial distinction is between the role and the role occupant; the role exists as something quite independent of the individual who currently happens to fill that role.

The concept of role, therefore, not only links the individual personality to the organisation, it also links the structural and dynamic processes of organisations.

RELATIONSHIPS INVOLVING TWO PEOPLE ONLY

The most simple form of relationship is a *two-way* interactive process (see Figure 4). Assuming a simple relationship between A and B, one could analyse:

(a)   the structure of the two positions

(b)   the conceptions A and B both have of their own role

(c)   the expectations A and B have of each other's role

(d)   the sanctions (rewards and punishments) which each
      may use to ensure compliance from the other.

One of the most universally applicable examples of a two-
person relationship is, of course, the marriage partnership.
Both spouses will have ideas not only about how they themselves want to behave, but also about how they want the other
spouse to behave. More importantly, there is a wide range of
options available to one spouse who seeks to change the
behaviour of the other; that is, a wide range of sanctions which
can be used to ensure the other's compliance.

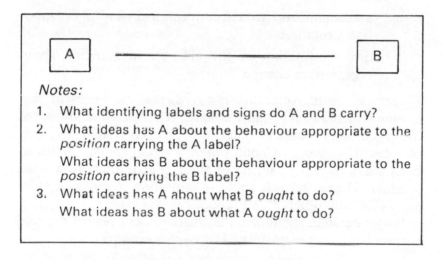

Figure 4
A simple model – the two-person relationship

ROLE ANALYSIS

The concept of role and the techniques of role analysis are
helpful in understanding and interpreting the patterns of
organisation and social behaviour. They enable the prediction
of behaviour and hence help the individual to act accordingly.
    The basic question for any public relations organisation is:
what can be done to reduce the incidence of role conflict and
ambiguity, and to make the effects of these conditions (when

they cannot be avoided) the least damaging to the person and to the organisation? The range of possibilities to be considered is as follows:

1. Introduce direct structural changes into the organisation.

2. Introduce new criteria of selection and placement.

3. Increase the tolerance and coping qualities of individuals.

4. Strengthen the personal bonds among members of the organisation.

All four of these possibilities would be facilitated by:

(a) a substantial revision of conventional views of organisation structure;

(b) direct utilisation of the role set in bringing about organisation change.

Formal organisation charts do not give a realistic representation of how organisations actually behave. A preferred definition of the organisation would be in terms of an open system, a system of roles. It consists of continuing, interdependent cycles of behaviour, related in terms of their contribution to a joint product. Hence, no role in an organisation is intact or fully separable from others (see Figure 5).

It is suggested, therefore, that management regard the role set as a basic unit of analysis. Hence, for example:

1. To change the behaviour of an individual or the content of his role requires a complementary change in the expectations of others in his role set.

2. Plans to change behaviour should be directed at the natural group, not at the individual in isolation from his role set.

3. Changes should only be introduced if there is awareness of the implications for all members of the role set.

STRESS FROM ROLE CONFLICT AND AMBIGUITY

Contradictory role expectations for the focal person give rise to

Figure 5
Three views of organisation structure

Notes:

Assume that an issue has arisen involving the performance and task requirements for position C6, one of 16 jobs at the first level of supervision in the organisation:

—— 1. Conventional organisation chart/approaches to management would regard this as an issue to be settled between the immediate supervisor and the subordinate whose job is at issue, viz B2 and C6.

– – – 2. The theory of overlapping group structures would see this issue as involving two 'organisation families', primarily within the group consisting of supervisor B2 and subordinates C5, C6, C7 and C8; secondarily between C6 and his own subordinates, D21, D22, D23 and D24.

...... 3. To approach the same problem in terms of the role set, we would begin by identifying the role set for position C6, ie to include those other people who have expectations of the behaviour of C6 and who communicate these expectations to C6.

These expectations of role senders ought to be *taken into account* in any process of evaluating and seeking to change the behaviour of C6. This does not of course necessarily require the meeting of all members of this role set to discuss every *issue* involving C6.

To illustrate: The activities of the person in role C6 will be affected not only by his/her expectations and those of his/her immediate boss, but also by the expectations of the person in position 1, the managing director. Particularly important for role C6 is the fact that the managing director too will have a direct relationship with his/her clients, X and Y in the diagram.

role conflicts. These conflicts generally have the following effects on the focal person: they intensify internal conflicts; they increase tension associated with various aspects of the job; they reduce satisfaction with the job; and they decrease confidence in superiors and in the organisation as a whole.

The strain involved in such conflict situations leads to various 'coping' responses; for example, social and psychological withdrawal. This response is damaging not only to the relationship between the individuals concerned, but potentially to the organisation as well, since the typical response to the stressful situation is to reduce communication and collaboration with the role sender.

Role ambiguity exists when the information available to a person is less than is required for adequate performance of his role. It is useful to distinguish between two types of role ambiguity:

(a)   task ambiguity: this results from lack of *definition* of the role. Its consequences are dissatisfaction with the job and feelings of futility.

(b)   socio-emotional ambiguity: this is where ambiguity exists about the individual's *evaluation* by other people. This type of ambiguity causes increased tension in the individual, and undermines both his own self-confidence and his trust in his colleagues.

Role ambiguity appears, from the research findings, to be a prevalent condition in modern organisations. It is fostered by the rapid pace of technological change and the complexities of modern organisations.

Some roles are necessarily more stressful than others. For example, people in innovative roles within bureaucratic organisations are subject to much pressure by other people in the organisation to maintain the status quo.

Similarly, people occupying boundary spanning roles (ie where the role set of the focal person extends to cover role senders both inside and outside the organisation) will often be subject to conflicting expectations; these expectations are often difficult to predict and to control, and people occupying roles at the boundary often have the additional problem of limited power resources at their disposal. Specifically, they are likely to be unclear about (a) their responsibilities, (b) where they fit into the organisation, (c) who they can legitimately influence, and (d) who has formal authority over them.

One point needs to be emphasised. We have discussed the negative effects of the stress which arises from both role ambiguity and role conflict, but this is not to imply that all ambiguity and conflict is necessarily counterproductive. On the contrary, a certain level of stress is healthy, both for the individual and for the organisation; it can promote creativity and innovativeness, both of which are vital to the public relations industry. The problem is to identify and maintain the optimum level of stress within the organisation, bearing in mind that individual personalities differ markedly in their ability to tolerate and benefit from stress.

CASE STUDY

Such a description of the theory behind role analysis is necessarily abstract, and so is best developed in the context of a practical example. This organisation has been chosen from the research material because its central problem is common to a great many public relations concerns: survival through and coping with the critical transitional phase in company development from the initial, pioneering stage of entrepreneurial activity, to the later stages of specialisation and integration. This transitional phase marks the critical turning point in the career of the entrepreneur. At this point he must decide either to stand still (which strategy may in fact prove impossible) or to opt for the alternative path of continued development, which will require him properly to organise his company. Many of the lessons to be drawn from this case apply just as much to the effective structuring of roles within an in-house operation.

As Figure 6 clearly illustrates, recent changes within the Chairman/Chief Executive's role set had effectively altered the balance between the two constituent parts of this role. Of all his relationships, those with people outside the organisation had increased as a proportion of the total. The implication of this was that the structural balance would shift towards the role of Chairman, and away from the role of Chief Executive. The role had become even more of a boundary spanning one; according to

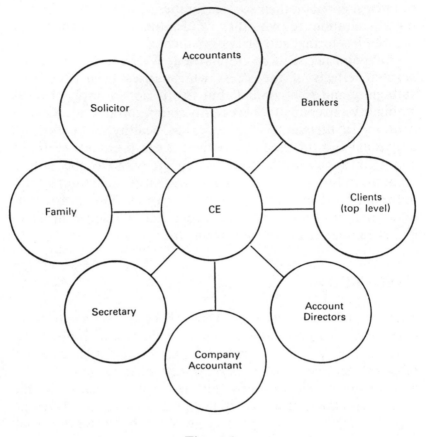

Figure 6
Case study: changing roles

(a) Current role of Chairman/Chief Executive

the theoretical arguments outlined earlier, we should expect an increase in the level of ambiguity under such conditions.

Previously all members of staff had related to the Chairman/Chief Executive on a one-to-one basis. This situation had since been improved by the channelling of relationships with Account Executives through the Account Director. Nevertheless, it is clear that the poor lateral communications within the company had developed precisely because of the previous direct lines of contact, from all staff to the Chairman/Chief Executive.

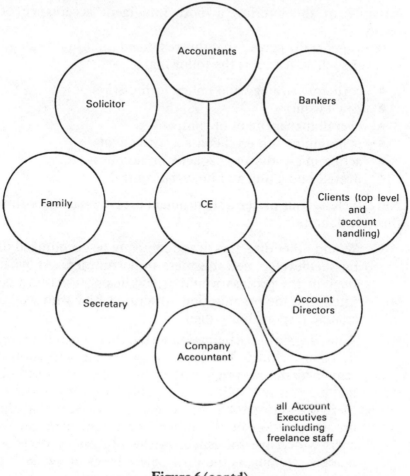

Figure 6 (contd)

(b) Previous role of Chairman/Chief Executive

Changes within the role set had provided a new *structure* for the role of the Chairman/Chief Executive. But the actual role can of course only develop if *behaviour* changes accordingly.

At this time, considerable ambiguity surrounded the development of this role. Basically, the ambiguity centred on the issue of whether the man at the top was simply Chairman or Chairman *and* Chief Executive of the company. It was felt that the metamorphosis from actively involved entrepreneur to Chairman was too drastic and hence not a viable proposition, and that the redefinition of the role as Chief Executive would be, certainly in the interim, a more intelligent acceptance of reality.

It was generally agreed that this redefined role would extend to cover such activities as the following:

- corporate strategy and policy formulation
- new business
- overall management of company
- maintaining top level contact with clients
- acting in an advisory capacity on accounts
- overall budgeting and financial control.

Nevertheless, four discernible problem areas remained within this role definition:

1. Would other directors of the company be encouraged to pursue/develop new business opportunities? At what stage of the process would a new business venture be fitted into the organisation structure? And who would assume responsibility then?

2. What degree of participation would there be in top level decision making? The locus of ownership and control remained the proprietor; the power base for decision making was not split as in a public company and was therefore very strong. Moreover, it was clear that the unique position of the proprietor would continue to exert a decisive influence on the process of decision making, so long as the dual power bases of ownership and control were concentrated in this way.

Two points should be made here:

(a) The decision making process involves a number of different, overlapping stages. While a proprietor (or indeed a director of public relations) may typically insist on the right finally to decide to complete the decision making process by choosing among the available options, nevertheless there is much scope for involvement of other directors throughout the earlier stages in the process. And it is naive indeed to underestimate the influence of, for example, information inputs and reasoned arguments on that process.

(b)   Basically any organisation at this stage of its development must decide what sort of organisation structure
it wishes to take as its model. Specifically, whether to
remain essentially an entrepreneurial activity or
whether instead to become a typical professional
management structure (see Figure 7). And of course
the basic principles underpinning that strategic
choice apply similarly to the development of an
in-house operation as much as to an external agency.

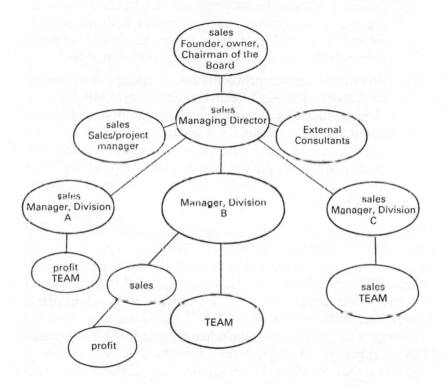

Note: Divisional split based on either functions or product/client/type of business

Figure 7
A typical 'professional management' structure

3.   Clients continued to expect the top man to be au fait with
the day-to-day running of their particular account. This
caused problems when such expectations conflicted with
those of account directors and executives (and indeed

those of the top man himself) who would like to have seen increased delegation. One solution was for the Chairman/Chief Executive to be kept informed by his staff to a reasonable level of detail, but for it to be clearly understood that this communication was essentially one-way; ie it should not provide a basis for dialogue, still less dissension, between the Chairman/Chief Executive and the director or executive concerned.

A second strategy was to modify the expectations involved. Where the subordinate's expectations regarding greater delegation were congruent with the preferences of the Chief Executive, it was the clients' expectations which, so far as possible, should be modified.

4. Potentially serious problems could have resulted where the Chairman/Chief Executive made a commitment to a client, which a subordinate then had to implement. This could put the subordinate in an untenable position. The solution lay in some role negotiation between the two people involved, the success of which depended on the ability of each to modify the expectations and hence behaviour of the other.

One point above all to emphasise is the interdependence of roles and role behaviour. Any given role will influence and in its turn be determined by the behaviour of other significant individuals. Hence, for example, in this case study, successful development of the Chairman's role was dependent upon appropriate developments in the role of his No. 2, but those were, in turn, contingent upon the Chairman's learning to delegate responsibility. Equally, developing the effective role of the No. 2 required that changes be made in his relationships with co-directors, and indeed between those co-directors and the top man.

The key point for creative public relations operations is to establish a sufficiently tight control on creative output to be able to ensure that the quality of advice and implementation remains intact.

In many UK public relations operations the loss of top level control has led to a rapid turnover of staff and clients. They have had difficulty in structuring themselves so as to maintain high quality service to clients *and* loyalty among staff.

DIAGNOSING PROBLEMS BY ROLE ANALYSIS

It is especially true in public relations that any given attitude or action can have far-reaching repercussions throughout the organisation and beyond it. In the simple two-person relationship, A's behaviour is determined partly by B's expectations; so, to achieve any change in A's behaviour, it is essential that at the same time B's expectations also change. In the case study above, the Chief Executive could only distance himself successfully from the day-to-day running of client accounts if, at the same time, there was a complementary change in the degree of involvement clients expected from him. Furthermore, behaviour and relationships are constantly changing, and the dynamic aspects must be sensitively appreciated.

It is helpful to look at public relations organisations as a series of interrelated roles. The conventional organisation chart (see Figure 5) gives no clues to the informal workings of the organisation, ignores the consequences of each individual's behaviour on everybody else, and by taking a snapshot in time and projecting this forward, assumes a stability which is not realistic.

The exercise in role analysis set out in Appendix 3 is much more useful as a diagnostic tool. It effectively produces an *audit* of role relationships within the organisation, and as such can be used for both initial evaluation and subsequent review purposes. It identifies the potential problem areas.

The public relations management task is to remedy any problems and deficiencies which are identified. The critical theoretical point is that roles are interdependent. *Translated into practical terms, this means that any attempt to change roles and role behaviour must be a two-way negotiating process.* This applies of course both within the public relations organisation and in the work undertaken by public relations practitioners. It becomes particularly relevant in the communications audit work done increasingly by public relations practitioners.

THE PROCESS OF ROLE DEFINITION

The process of role definition, applied to the organisation discussed in the case study above, can be set out as follows:

1. Comprehensive listing of all tasks
2. Identify tasks which are:
    - clearly the chairman's role
    - clearly the managing director's role   individually
    - potential areas of conflict
3. Discuss role definitions
4. Discuss conflict resolution   together
5. Revise role definitions

To be effective, role definitions must be worked out participatively. They must also be flexible, adaptive and constantly under review. They must be explicitly defined and above all well communicated. It is therefore a necessary first step in the process for each person involved to be perfectly clear themselves on what they are prepared to negotiate over and what they are not. Following are a few initial suggestions for guiding the redefinitions:

Areas over which the Chairman maintains personal control

1. Overall budgeting and financial control
2. Distribution of profits
3. Allocation of resources among divisions
4. Corporate strategy and policy formulation
5. Structure and functioning of the Board
6. Vetting of new business opportunities/proposals
7. Top level contacts (social) with all clients
8. Direct contact with bankers, legal advisors etc
9. Direct contact with top decision makers in business, politics, the media
10. Acting in an advisory capacity (creative counselling)
11. Ultimate resolution of disputes between subordinates
    How far down the organisational hierarchy should this extend?

Role of the Managing Director

1. Responsible for overall profitability

2. Responsible for integration of various divisions so as to ensure coherent functioning and efficient resource allocation

3. Responsible for maintaining quality control, and providing Chairman with evaluative comments on the effectiveness of campaigns

4. Responsible for regular (three-monthly?) staff appraisals to be discussed with (a) Chairman? (b) Chairman and person concerned? (c) person concerned only?

5. Responsible for staff development

Potential areas of conflict

1. Allocation of resources among divisions

2. Evaluation of divisional performance

3. Personnel policies

4. To what extent is/should the company be personified by the Chairman/founder?

5. Seeking out new business opportunities

6. Organisation within the company of new business ventures

7. Top level client contact: (a) to what extent should the Chairman be briefed about clients' accounts? (b) to what extent can/should the Chairman be able to commit the company?

Role of the Board and the Management Group

The definition of the roles of the Board and the Management Group must be made within the following parameters:

1. The Board has both legal and organisational responsibilities; the Management Group's responsibility is primarily to the company.

2. The roles of both the Board and the Management Group need to be precisely defined to remove ambiguity. But these groups should not be constituted in an excessively rigid or inflexible way, particularly since most people hold joint membership of both groups.

3. The (authority) relationships which need to be precisely defined are as follows:

    (a) the relationship between the Board and the Management Group

    (b) the relationship between the Board and the Chairman and Managing Director/principal shareholder

    (c) the relationship between the Management Group and the other members of the organisation.

Role of the Board

1. Responsible for long-term thinking and planning – ie corporate strategy

2. Responsible for setting overall company objectives and for evaluating/reviewing overall company performance matched against those objectives

    Objectives can be simple (eg that the company should aim for a certain level of total fee income, or for a certain return on investment) or they may be wider in scope (eg to include company philosophy toward personnel). Whatever the formal objectives, it is essential that (a) there is agreement among the directors over the objectives, and (b) these objectives are clearly communicated to all members of the organisation so as to achieve a feeling of real involvement at all levels in the organisation.

Role of the Management Group

1. More operational than the Board. Responsible for short-term activity/planning – ie tactics, making operational the corporate objectives defined by the Board

2. Responsible for continuous monitoring of performance as matched against objectives

3. Effective functioning requires good integration between constituent members, information sharing, high level of openness and trust, positive attitude toward problem solving.

It is suggested that the best possible way to define the role and terms of reference of the Board and the Management Group is by agreement of those involved. A possible way to proceed is for all those involved independently to draft their own definitions, and for these then to be discussed in a meeting. Out of such discussion an agreed definition should emerge.

THE PR ROLES AS SEEN BY PRACTITIONERS

Difficult and easy relationships

Before analysing and seeking to explain the relative difficulties of working with various groups, it is obviously necessary to identify those groups. This in itself is often not the simple task it might seem to be.

It is hard to say which in terms of groups represent the toughest . . . I suppose the toughest thing is to define those groups.

First, there is the problem that particular target audiences may conceal great diversity. It may not be possible to find a common approach to communicating with this disparate audience sector. Second, although identification of the group may not be difficult, it may be hard to establish communication links.

You can develop channels of communication on the back of some obvious business link or common interest, but if the common interest does not appear to be there then you have to try and make bricks without straw.

So, for example,

. . . there is no immediate platform that I can think of for talking to the TUC as such. On an individual basis we think there is some sort of platform like saying to the TUC General Secretary, Len Murray: 'You are an influential man. Why don't we talk?' (I would regard him as very much a moderate in the trade union movement, somebody who likes to think of himself as accessible.) I think that is the problem – although we see the TUC or members of the unions as opinion formers there is not a natural platform for our industry to talk to the TUC. We are not unionised in this company; it might be slightly different if we were. So I do not think there is any natural platform. I would have thought that this is something a lot of companies have difficulty with.

So far as external relations are concerned, it seems that most difficulties will arise where there is no natural platform for dialogue, where no channels of communication exist.

> The EEC, I think, is the most difficult . . . because it is a growing bureaucracy.

Ironically, while some may assert that internal relations are the most straightforward to deal with ('because we are in control of what we say . . . you cannot control what is going to be in the *Financial Times* tomorrow, you can only do your best'), a more typical reaction reverses the problem.

> I believe that there is some misunderstanding between management and its staff in a vast organisation – and I am not necessarily confining myself to my own industry – than in almost any other field. We are not going to be able to progress in industry in this country, I am absolutely certain, without a complete and thorough understanding of all the tensions and pressures and understandings which are necessary between us and our staff.

> Internal communications are the biggest problem of all.

But the problem is more than simply a question of inadequate communications, and hence its resolution is much harder.

> This lack of trust is not through lack of endeavour on our part, or lack of endeavour on their part, but they sometimes believe that we are doing things which are not in the best interests of the industry, and we believe that they *are* being done in the best interests of the industry. It is difficult sometimes to meet these different points of view.

This is of course an inherent dilemma. The best interests of the industry might not necessarily coincide with the best interests of the unions. Indeed, this is the rationale behind using the stakeholder model to analyse how organisations function: the various interest groups all have different objectives which may compete and even conflict.

> We have to find ways of bridging that gap. I do not see this as an easy task, and anyone who thinks that it is an easy task, in my judgement, is deluding himself.

And, in terms of the arguments presented in Chapter 1, this surely is precisely the increasingly critical role of public relations.

Role ambiguity

Regardless of specific activity, ambiguity about what one is doing or ought to be doing is as potent a source of anxiety and stress as work overload.

> As far as workload is concerned, I do not have a problem. If I have stacks and stacks of things to do, fine, I just get on with it. I do not find that bothers me. But I do find that what you have described as the ambiguity of the situation or the lack of knowledge as to what is possibly required in some circumstances is a difficult one, yes.

Public relations is currently an ambiguous function; the discussion in Chapter 1 illustrates this clearly. Whether such ambiguity is inherent in the very nature of public relations activity, or whether this is simply an historical observation at this stage in its development as a discipline, remains a matter for conjecture. What is clear is that PR practitioners, inside organisations and operating independently, have in hand a significant public relations exercise on their own behalf.

> One feels uncertain what other people expect from PR. The parameters are very difficult to lay down. It is a largely subjective thing in many people's minds as to how you make up your mind whether you should be putting anything at all in this area. If so, how much, so, what recipient should you choose for your favours? It is difficult.

Conflict

Perhaps surprisingly, it seems to be the ambiguity of the public relations function which gives rise to conflicts of opinion. Frequently such disagreements focus on the cost effectiveness of public relations activities (whether the ends justify the means, ie costs) rather than technical disagreement over the means themselves.

> I suppose you would find some of our more earnest senior management might raise an eyebrow, saying: 'Why do we spend so much time on things like that?' But it is all a coating on the pill.

Where there are conflicts over the actual carrying out of the public relations function, these tend to centre round the issue of when to react and when not to react. Opinions on this frequently derive from individuals' particular areas of responsibilities; they are functional rather than just attitudinal differences of opinion. Any solution must therefore seek to resolve a

basic conflict of interests. For example: the public relations
director of a nationalised industry described his biggest problem area as his relationship with the industry's 'legal people'.
He believes very strongly in giving people the facts so that they
may make up their own minds: 'It is a slow process of influence
. . . very, very slow.' In contrast, the legal department prefers
to disclose no information unless absolutely essential; to keep
their arguments guarded until decisions are made, inquiries
have reported, or legislation has been passed. Similarly, the
public relations head of an international bank advocates
'speedy, honest, accurate' handling of any problem as soon as it
emerges. Typically, branch managers of the bank, or managing
directors of subsidiaries, are reluctant to do this: 'I do not want
to divulge that information at the moment because I will not be
able to resolve that problem.'

Most public relations practitioners advocate a straightforward and efficient approach to dealing with problems as they
arise, the basic philosophy being that to attempt to conceal the
truth is, in the end, very probably a misguided strategy. The
critical quality though seems to be the ability to judge
accurately just when to react and when not to. 'I think, on
balance, if you are in doubt you should not respond.' But this
judgement can, of course, only be developed through experience.

Influence

Public relations is essentially seen as a support service, and so
practitioners have to work through persuasion. 'The professional challenge is how effective your persuasion is.' To a large
extent, the effectiveness of the public relations man's attempts to
influence will be determined by his own personal credibility.

> One's credibility builds up over a period of time and once you
> have a track record behind you people will trust you and they
> will accept your judgement. Earlier on it is very, very difficult,
> and that is why you see, I think, PR people in and out of jobs
> after a year or so, because they have come to a head-on collision.
> They have not had time to build up credibility before the crisis
> and then advice has been counter to what the management
> believes necessary, and out they go. Provided you have managed
> to build up that credibility and you have handled mini-crises
> effectively, even against the advice of the management, you

have done it in the way which you know is right, then when the big one comes they will stand back. I have already passed through that transition.

STRESS

There are many potential causes of individual stress within organisations. As we have seen, stress can be produced in situations where there is either ambiguity or conflict about what a person is meant to be doing and how he is or is not doing it. It is obvious that work overload can produce a high level of stress, but what is less generally appreciated is that work underload can become just as stressful for the individual. In fact, it is possible to identify the optimum workload, where the individual feels sufficiently enthusiastic and motivated to perform at his best. When the level of pressure increases markedly beyond this, it becomes a problem, and anxiety begins to diminish his performance. Equally, when the level of pressure is significantly reduced, he feels less need to perform well (or ultimately at all); his work suffers and he feels increasingly dissatisfied and finally alienated and depressed.

Obviously the optimum level of stress varies between people and, indeed, the same person may be able to tolerate different levels of stress over time.

This introduces another interesting dimension which is still being researched. Assume that Mr A has found that he performs best when he is under a certain amount of pressure – which we shall call level X. Suppose he has one major problem on his mind which is making him feel stressed. Will the effects of this be more serious, less serious or the same as if he were worrying about several, smaller problems? Cumulatively, would these equal the big problem?

This diversity of stress sources is one of the most significant characteristics of the public relations role. He is in an invidious position. He stands between the organisation and the world outside. He is responsible to both for interpreting the other's perceptions. He has relatively little influence on shaping events but is often held responsible for many of the consequences of those events. His programmed routine is constantly punctuated by series of crises – mini or otherwise. Most managers deplore what they call 'interruptions' in their day. The public relations man does not have the word 'interruption' in his vocabulary; eruptions are the stuff of his job.

> To be a good PR man you have to be able to leave what you are doing and come back and almost pick it up at the full stop that you left it. It is an attitude of mind – a sort of grasshopper mind.

The public relations man is always in a stressful position, with continual pressure from a diversity of sources; and at the same time he has to cope with the extra pressure produced whenever one particularly critical issue erupts.

The public relations function is essentially a support service, an advisory function. The position of all staff specialists within an organisation makes them vulnerable to high levels of anxiety and stress. Research shows that they are becoming increasingly concerned about their credibility with line management; public relations has a special problem in proving its effectiveness to a sceptical management.

THE RELATIONSHIP BETWEEN INDIVIDUAL AND ORGANISATION STRESS

A crisis has been defined in terms of individual stress levels among key executives reaching a peak, and so becoming an organisation phenomenon (see Chapter 7). Clearly there is a delicate balance between stress at the individual level and at the organisation level. The response of the public relations man is critical here, for to a large degree he is responsible for constraining the possible mushrooming of any stress which does exist within the organisation.

To illustrate: financial crises are frequently recognised inside companies up to twelve months prior to public announcement (twelve months being the period for disclosure of financial information). Clearly this is an attempt to stem the onset of a vicious circle of falling confidence. Similarly, abstracting from the individual to the organisation level, in situations of *underload* the organisation becomes complacent, unable to innovate or produce creative solutions.

COPING WITH STRESS

It is clear that stress at an optimum level is helpful for the effective working of both individuals and the organisation overall; that where the optimum level of stress on an individual is exceeded there is a real danger that the stress will mushroom and become an organisation problem; and that stress can emanate from the very structure itself, as well as from the individual personality.

Where the source of the stress is structural, obviously structural solutions can be implemented. The range of possibilities for dealing with role ambiguity, role legitimation conflict and role activation conflict have already been considered in this chapter. Where the source is personal, people develop their own special ways of coping. The best advice is for people to try to analyse for themselves precisely what causes them to feel stressed, and to try some of the solutions advocated by others.

There is self-imposed pressure, one is impatient. We all strive for perfection. I retreat, I have a cottage, I cut myself off from it. I am a devotee of the opera: once a week, inside Covent Garden, there is no world existing outside. It is a form of escape.

Sometimes the very thing that gets you away from the doldrums of fretting about it is another problem.

Now and again I have drinks in the evening with my Chairman or the Director General. We sit and chat. I find this satisfying in so far as it is a bit uplifting. You think, I have got problems, but he has much more at the moment on his plate, and look how he is coping.

Discussing things with civilised people is in itself an outlet.

I do not get terrible gut-turning feelings in this job. Generally speaking, I find the thing that most cuts me up is when I have major disagreements with my colleagues.

Stress is a very good word! The PR man is often in an untenable position, the demands of internal and external (in banking) are so opposing. He is trying to bring the two together, so he is the crossroads. That does create pressure and stress. You can cope by structuring the situation. If it is not possible to make a public statement – I have great faith in the leading financial, economic and political journalists – I often advise them of what is happening on an off-the-record basis, saying that they may hear some rumour of this event, I will tell them what it is now, but it is not to be divulged. So I keep lines of communication open on a private basis.

Chapter 4

Organisation Culture and the Individual in PR

The idea of 'role' links the individual person into the organisation in which he lives, works or plays.

Previous discussion has shown that the role of public relations as a management activity is frequently ambiguous. This applies whether we are talking about its objectives, its methods, its value and usefulness, or even its ethics. So any individual in public relations inevitably lives and works in an ambiguous context. There are, of course, both advantages and disadvantages in this. Ambiguity is for some people tantamount to freedom; other people find ambiguous situations very stressful. From the organisation's point of view, it is necessary to maintain the delicate balance between the minimum level of control and formalisation needed for the effective working of the organisation as a whole, and allowing individuals sufficient scope and flexibility to realise their full potential in terms of creativity and innovative thinking.

Organisations vary in the way in which they perceive and attempt to strike this balance. The two extremes have been described. Bureaucratic organisations allow little flexibility to the individual; roles are explicitly defined; control, authority and communication are hierarchical. In contrast, organismic or non-bureaucratic organisations allow much more individual freedom; tasks and roles are continually updated and redefined as the need arises; control, authority and communication are based on a network pattern of relationships.

These extremes can be developed, using additional dimensions, to give characterisations, if not caricatures, of organisations and the people living and working in them. The important point is that individuals have natural preferences for different

59

types of organisation, which have been described as 'organisation idealogies' (Harrison) and as 'organisational cultures' (Handy). According to Handy, there are four possible cultures: the power culture, the role culture, the task culture and the person culture.

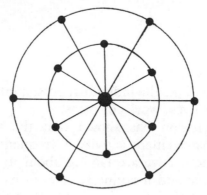

Figure 8
The Power Culture: (Zeus, God of Gods)

Source: Handy (1976)

THE POWER CULTURE

A spider's web is used to illustrate power culture (see Figure 8). The locus of power and control is held firmly in the centre, which has direct connections to all functions and specialisms throughout the organisation. This is the opposite of bureaucracy; there are few rules and regulations, instead control is by personal authority.

Usually, small entrepreneurial organisations have a power culture. As such, they can make decisions and react quickly and effectively in the face of change. This is why small businesses are often surprisingly adept at surviving under rapidly changing or turbulent conditions. Whether or not the responses made are the most appropriate ones depends entirely on the calibre of the person at the centre. Clearly, this is a potential source of weakness, and indeed many successful family firms plunge into decline when founding fathers are succeeded by foundling sons.

The other limitation is that the power culture's very structure imposes a constraint on growth. Increasing size must lead to decentralised decision making, control by rules and procedures, ie the antithesis of the power culture. The spider's web may collapse under the strain. Many entrepreneurial organisations in fact grow by spawning satellites. All have a high degree of autonomy, linked only in some financial relationship (eg a requirement to yield a specified return on investment. (Slater Walker, GEC and John Bentley's enterprises all operated on this principle.)

Charles Handy caricatures his organisation cultures by referring to the gods of Greek mythology. The power culture is 'proud and strong' and calls to mind Zeus, 'the all-powerful head of the Gods of Ancient Greece who ruled by whim and impulse, by thunderbolt and shower of gold from Mount Olympus'. Such cultures are concerned with results rather than means and can be seen as ruthless. They provide the ideal setting for the competitive, ambitious and able person who is clearly determined to fight his way to the top, but middle management can feel very powerless, and a high turnover rate at this level is typical.

THE ROLE CULTURE

A role culture (see Figure 9) is basically a bureaucracy. Handy

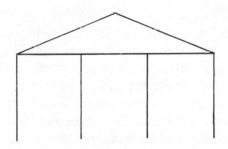

Figure 9
The Role Culture: (Apollo, God of good order)

Source: Handy (1976)

sees this as analogous with the clearly defined structure of a Greek temple, whose patron god is Apollo, the god of reason. For the underlying principles of the role culture are logic and rationality.

The strength of the Greek temple lies in its pillars, and its pillars are very strong: the different departments and specialisms. This kind of organisation is very effective under stable conditions but, as Handy has it, 'Greek temples are insecure when the ground shakes'. And indeed many large organisations with this kind of culture faced problems during the turbulent 1960s. For there are inadequate links between the pillars, except at the level of the pediment – a narrow band of senior management – and successful intregration is of course critical if the organisation is to adapt to cope with change.

Within a role culture, greater importance is often attached to the job description rather than to how the particular individual fills it. Similarly, influence is through rules and procedures rather than any kind of personal authority. Fromm describes bureaucratic individuals and, clearly, whichever direction the causal chain (ie whether bureaucracies develop bureaucratic personalities or whether bureaucratic people select each other and stick together and operate organisations bureaucratically) only these kind of people are going to be effective and happy in such a culture. Role cultures are safe, secure, predictable and perhaps, too respectable. Bureaucratic life offers few surprises – good or bad.

The task culture

Most managers at middle and junior levels would, given the choice, prefer to work toward the performing of a task or project (see Figure 10). In small and medium-sized organisations, ad hoc working groups and project teams are established specifically to carry out a given task. This is often the case in well established, behaviourally aware organisations in fields such as advertising, public relations, design and management consulting. Such groups are set up for a clear reason, and can be abandoned or re-established as the need arises. Groups tend naturally toward entropy where the central task has been completed or otherwise disappeared, and cease to exist except

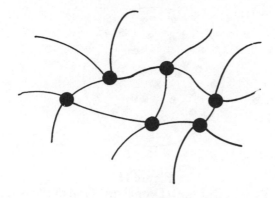

Figure 10
The Task Culture
Source: Handy (1976)

in situations where they are kept almost unnaturally alive by fossilisation of their organisation. It is or should be clear to everyone working in a particular division that their responsibilities, loyalties and energies are directed toward achieving that division's task.

Handy comments that this culture has no totally appropriate 'presiding deity, perhaps because the Ancients were more interested in style and principle and power than in performance'. He sees the task culture as a *net*, with some strands thicker and stronger than others. Power and influence lie at the interstices of the net, at the knots, and derive from expertise rather than position or personality. Each work group operates with a high degree of autonomy, and since decision making can then be directed solely toward achieving the group's objective this type of culture is satisfactory from the point of view of both the organisation and the individual. Top management controls by allocating resources amongst the various groups, but it cannot exert more detailed day-to-day control over what actually goes on. It only has control over the output which, in terms of the ends/means distinction illustrated in Figure 2.4, may well encourage innovation. But problems arise when resources are limited and groups must compete and politic for their share.

63

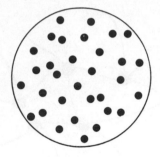

Figure 11
The Person Culture: (Dioneisus, God of Pleasure)

THE PERSON CULTURE

Person cultures (see Figure 11) are, in the pure form, unusual. The focus is the individual; and people will only develop some form of organisation, or subscribe to an already existing one, to the extent that it serves to further their own interests. Professional partnerships and of course many social groups, including families, are person cultures in this sense.

Structure in such cultures is minimal. Control is difficult since people like this will only accept whatever external control they choose to accept. Handy calls such structures Dionysian, after the god of the self-oriented individual and 'the first existentialist'. It is the perversity of organisations that they do tend to develop their own momentum, and as soon as this happens of course the individuals reject their legitimacy.

It should be self-evident that most individuals who have opted to work in public relations would find a role culture incompatible with their personal preferences. Neither would such an organisation be very effective in this type of industry. Equally, a person culture is almost impossible to manage, and where there is direct and immediate feedback from a range of clients, as is the case in public relations, this is probably not a viable option. Consequently most public relations firms begin as power cultures, where everyone is happy to start with, especially the power baron, but then middle-level executives

64

become disillusioned and move off – often to start their own spider's web. If the company can, however, successfully manage to grow in size, it is most likely to develop a task culture, and as already pointed out, this is precisely how the bigger consultancies are organised.

Chapter 5
Performance

One of the most critical issues in the management of public relations is how to define and evaluate performance. Indeed, many would argue that this is the key problem area in public relations management, and that the special problems faced by PR men serve to distinguish this from many other types of management activity.

Evaluation is essential, not only so that comparisons can be made with other organisations, but also as part of the learning process which any organisation must go through to improve its understanding of the differences between desired and actual results.

The concept of performance needs to be clearly understood before any attempt can be made to develop measures with which to evaluate it. But a satisfactory definition is very hard to come by. Most attempts at definition have been limited to consideration of performance in economic terms. This approach completely ignores all other facets of organisation performance: attitudes, perceptions, beliefs, motivations, habits and expectations of human beings.

Even if we accept this limited way of looking at performance, there remains a considerable problem in the selection of a satisfactory economic measure, which is applicable across different organisations and industrial sectors. Any chosen indicator of economic performance must be identified with some specific corporate goal. It will not be capable of taking into account, for instance, the different perspectives of shareholders and management towards the measurement of economic performance.

The very real problems surrounding the measurement of

performance have in fact been exacerbated by a failure first to formulate a precise definition.

RECENT ATTEMPTS TO MEASURE PERFORMANCE

Using data from a cross-section of UK companies, Samuels and Smythe examined:

(a) the behaviour of profit rates and the variability of profit rates in relation to size of company;

(b) the relation between industrial concentration and variability of profit rates.

They presented the following conclusions:

1. Profit rates and firm size are inversely related.

2. There was a tendency for profit rates to fall over the period covered.

3. The time variability of profit rates and the group variability of profits are both inversely related to firm size.

4. Firms operating in highly concentrated industries have less variable profit rates than firms operating in less highly concentrated industries.

Samuels and Smythe measured company size on the basis of net assets, since this index is readily available from an analysis of company balance sheets. However, as they pointed out, this does not provide a totally satisfactory index, since (a) assets may not be properly valued, (b) some assets are valued on an historical cost basis, whereas other companies base asset values on replacement costs, (c) some companies are more capital-intensive than others. Alternative measures of company size are turnover and employment. Samuels and Smythe chose not to use these indicators; as such information is not compulsory, its use would have reduced their sample size. It is interesting to note that in fact the various available measures of firm size correlate closely with each other.

The measure of profitability used by Samuels and Smythe was the ratio of profits (after depreciation but before taxation) to net assets. This is the 'book yield on investment' which, despite difficulties in its use, gives the best approximation to the profitability of a company. It has been suggested that there is in fact no other way of measuring return on investment for a continuing company.

In his study of company performance, Child collected financial data on the following:

(a) *income*: ie gross trading profit less fees but before deducting depreciation; investment income added;

(b) *assets*: fixed assets net of depreciation, with current assets added and current liabilities deducted;

(c) *sales turnover*.

Child reiterates the remarks of Samuels and Smythe on the problems inherent in using net assets as a basis for comparisons across companies and industries. Hence, his main indicator of growth is restricted to a standardised score for sales growth.

The data presented in Child's paper do not indicate very strong relationships between company performance and the organisational variables studied. Child admits that this may reflect inadequacies in the measurement techniques used. More interestingly, he indicates the potential relevance of environmental factors for organisational performance. First, for example, there appear to be inter-industry differences in the relationship between size and performance, probably deriving from technological and market factors peculiar to different industries. Second, Child suggests that the concentration of ownership with control is not related to performance across the sample as a whole. Within the context of certain environments, the linking of interests of ownership and control may well affect survival and performance of the organisation.

It is precisely because organisations operate within environments which are peculiar to themselves that inter-company comparisons become so complex. Merrett and Lehr present an illuminating comparison of profitability between a sample of public and 'large' private companies, based on return on total assets (see Figure 12). Though they claim that this comparison is as accurate as is practically possible from published data, they make the point that no sensible comparison can be made between the performance of public and 'small' private companies 'since each is clearly specialising in areas in which they

Industry	Weighted Average Return on Total Assets %	
	Private Companies	*Public Companies*
Food	14.0	9.7
Drink	14.2	9.9
Chemicals	10.1	8.5
Metal manufacture	12.6	7.1
Non-electrical engineering	7.9	8.3
Electrical engineering	6.0	9.9
Other metal goods	13.1	10.5
Textiles	5.5	9.3
Clothing and footwear	10.2	9.3
Bricks, pottery and glass	10.8	10.5
Timber	9.5	8.5
Paper and printing	11.2	8.8
Other manufacturing	13.5	8.8
Construction	8.3	7.7
Transport	6.2	7.9

Source: Merrett and Lehr

Figure 12
Weighted mean return on total assets

do not overlap. . . . They have different comparative advantages.'

PIMS profit models

A research project was undertaken by the Marketing Science Institute of Harvard Business School, into the on-going profit impact of marketing strategies (PIMS). The objective of this research was to provide top management, corporate planners, marketing executives and divisional management with insights and information on expected profit performance of different kinds of businesses under different competitive conditions. The research specifically aimed to answer the following questions which arise in the process of strategic planning:

1. What rate of return on investment (ROI) is normal in a given type of business, under given market and industry conditions?

2. What factors explain the differences in typical levels of ROI among various kinds of businesses?

3. How will ROI in a specific business be affected by a change in strategy employed? By a change in competitive activity?

The PIMS research team constructed an equation which explained more than 80 per cent of the variation in profitability among the 620 businesses subsequently incorporated into the PIMS data base. This profit level equation includes more than 60 terms composed of various combinations of the 37 basic factors (see Figure 13). Together with a second equation, which explains *changes* in ROI, this formed the basis of separate diagnostic reports which were constructed for each company in the data pool. For example: it was now possible to determine an average relationship between market share and profitability by comparing average levels of ROI for groups of businesses with different market shares.

The individual diagnostic reports gave an analysis of the ROI for each company, showing how this was affected by each of the 37 factors in the equation. The report could then be used as a standard of performance not only at company level, but also between operating divisions. The most valuable application of the profit model was facilitating an analysis of the reasons for past performance, and hence providing pointers for the best directions for strategic changes. Certainly the PIMS profit models provided a valuable contribution to the measurement, in economic terms, of company performance, as this is determined by environmental influences.

PERFORMANCE IN PR

It is clear from the above discussion that daunting problems surround the defining of performance, especially the selection and use of appropriate measures. Even taking economic performance alone, no consensus emerges.

More than any other aspect of management, public relations defies attempts to derive a below-the-line figure for any given activity. While the basic philosophy and rationale behind

Return on investment (ROI)
The ratio of net, pretax operating income to average investment. Operating income is what is available after deduction of allocated corporate overhead expenses but before deduction of any financial charges on assets employed. 'Investment' equals equity plus long-term debt or, equivalently, total assets employed minus current liabilities attributed to the business.

Market share
The ratio of dollar sales by a business, in a given time period, to total sales by all competitors in the same market. The 'market' includes all of the products or services, customer types and geographic areas that are directly related to the activities of the business. For example, it includes all products and services that are competitive with those sold by the business.

Product (service) quality
The quality of each participating company's offerings, appraised in the following terms: What was the percentage of sales of products or services from each business in each year which were superior to those of competitors? What was the percentage of equivalent products? Inferior products?

Marketing expenditures
Total costs for sales force, advertising, sales promotion, marketing research and marketing administration. The figures do not include costs of physical distribution.

R and D expenditures
Total costs of product development and process improvements, including those costs incurred by corporate-level units which can be directly attributed to the individual business.

Investment intensity
Ratio of total investment to sales.

Corporate diversity
An index which reflects (a) the number of different four-digit Standard Industrial Classification industries in which a corporation operates, (b) the percentage of total corporate employment in each industry, and (c) the degree of similarity or difference among the industries in which it participates.

Source: Schoeffler, Buzzell and Heany

Figure 13
ROI and key profit influences

public relations are still so shrouded in confusion and ambiguity, attempts to define or measure its contribution are doomed. Is it the purpose of PR to create a situation where economic performance of the organisation is likely to be enhanced? Or is PR concerned with non-economic indicators: attitudes, perceptions, beliefs, motivations, habits, expectations? Is any concern with the latter seen merely as a strategic route to achieving the former, or are these things valued for themselves? If PR is concerned with economic facets of performance, must the search continue to try to find some way of giving a numerical – preferably financial – value to its contribution? If on the other hand PR is seen to be primarily concerned with the intervening variables – whether as a means to an economic end or as an end in itself – does it really matter that we cannot put a figure in below the line?

> I think that individual performance is more difficult to evaluate than company performance. I do not think company performance is that difficult. You can see the sort of impact you may be creating with the outside world, to some extent you can measure it – like people ringing you up and asking for your opinion, which presumably means you are worth listening to. That sort of thing is not too difficult. Certainly, on the back of advertising campaigns you can do a certain amount of measuring as to whether you are really getting through to people and whether your message is right.

Some PR practitioners stipulate that to be really effective, the ideas and concepts which they put forward must lead to changes in action. But of course this begs two questions. Firstly, it must be clearly evident that either some positive action has been taken or, conversely, some action has been averted. Secondly, that action/lack of action must be clearly attributable to the PR activity aimed at achieving that result. Obviously activities such as exhibitions or sponsored functions allow for this kind of evaluation. Similarly, effective PR handling can avert some of the negative effects and repercussions of, for example, labour disputes, or other types of crisis situations.

As a general rule, it is probably true to say that the effectiveness of PR is always difficult to demonstrate, and its cost difficult to justify, whether it is continuous or ad hoc.

> Sometimes senior management might consider that we go in for a few luxuries. . . . Some of our more earnest senior management

might raise on eyebrow, saying 'why do we spend so much time on things like that?' But it is all a coating on the pill. While they are reading about the beauty queen competition in the paper, they are also seeing stories about output and productivity, the results from various new machines, what we are doing in research – all this sort of thing is going in as well.

Such on-going activity may depend solely for its effectiveness on a change in what are called the intervening variables of organisation performance; changed perceptions, for example:

> We are now a profit making body who beat its contract by X million pounds in 1978. If you look in the Annual Report and Accounts we still get a contract worth something like Y million pounds from the Government to provide a service which is not profit making. So instead of being a company that loses Y million pounds, we are a company that beats the contract by X million pounds. That is a good enough proof, I would think, of the effectiveness of public affairs on the PR side.

But of course the effectiveness of any PR activity is heavily dependent upon a series of extraneous events and circumstances. 'You cannot control what the *Financial Times* prints'. Moreover, regardless of the merit of the PR effort, other news events may overshadow its significance.

> You can measure to some extent, but very often we do a superb job, and the result may be nothing in the newspaper, because something else more newsworthy has happened on the same day. Or we might have done a superb job in killing a rumour or a story which has no foundation in fact. I think we can only get satisfaction by asking ourselves the question: Did you do that well? And you develop personal standards and self criticism.

> Senior management colleagues might sometimes be disappointed because the results have not apparently justified the trouble they have taken, but when you explain to them that maybe something else of world importance has happened the same day or somebody else has made a similar announcement – as long as you can satisfy them that they have done everything that they could conceivably have done – they are content.

The evaluation of performance at the individual level is probably similarly more feasible where one is dealing with an organisation that has built-in procedures for monitoring activities, costs, budgets and whether the agreed message is reaching the target at the right time. But it is also true that in ad hoc situations, rather than on-going routine PR activity, an agreed measurement formula can be found. People can be evaluated for their efficiency, cooperation, affability and positive approach. The real challenges are presented by crisis situations.

> Obviously I evaluate my staff on their success in reaching their objectives, as my boss will evaluate my success in achieving my objectives. But also on their responsiveness to crisis situations. That is a strong word, 'crisis', but to situations which are not planned for, and the willingness to work at something, not to panic, not to flap; to help, to guide – all those things. So one must never forget that in public relations the personal element is very, very important. It is the ability to always respond. So responsiveness comes into my definition of their evaluation. But it becomes a very subjective thing.

A PROVEN APPROACH TO EVALUATING PR PERFORMANCE

The following approach to evaluating the performance of PR activity was initially developed for use within my own company, but subsequently I have found many of my clients enthusiastic.

I wanted to consider how to evaluate the effectiveness of client campaigns, bearing in mind the following criteria:

- time input
- deployment of my total resources
- creative input
- communication between the client organisation and the appropriate environment.

Regular and accurate evaluation of on-going client relationships would provide invaluable information, which could be used as a basis to improve relationships, and to increase the probabilities of that particular business being renewed.

It is advantageous when developing new business proposals, to be able to demonstrate to prospective clients that all relationships are regularly and systematically reviewed, and to explain the reasons for doing so. To facilitate a sophisticated evaluation procedure, three tools were developed:

(a) *checklist*, to evaluate objectively the effectiveness of client relationships;

(b) *questionnaire*, to elicit the client's subjective assessment of the relationship;

(c) *activity record*, to provide basic data for the objective evaluation, ie to be used as information input to the checklist.

Objective evaluation and review

There appear to be two aspects to the 'effectiveness' of any client relationship:

(a) from the point of view of the PR specialist/consultancy;

(b) from the point of view of the client.

Clearly the two aspects are closely related, but are not identical and hence should not be confused.

The PR specialist's criteria for 'effectiveness' are:

- no apparent indications of client dissatisfaction
- good prospects for renewal of the business
- profitability.

It may seem that client satisfaction would derive from an effective campaign, where effectiveness is objectively defined. To some extent this is so, but effectiveness from the client's point of view is substantially 'perceived' effectiveness.

The checklist in Appendix 3 was developed by taking a number of operational measures of effectiveness, and defining these as potential problem areas:

- time input
- costs
- clarity of role definition
- campaign effectiveness
- evaluation of creative input
- optimal deployment of resources
- implementation
- communication with the public.

The basic formula for measuring effectiveness is: given the process of public relations activity, has the output been satisfactory vis à vis the imput? Specialist departments and external consultancies alike need to be sensitive to all early indications of client dissatisfaction, and to react before that dissatisfaction can develop. The checklist in Appendix 3 facilitates this process.

Where appropriate, the checklist also facilitates a comparison between actual and budgeted/forecast figures (for example, time input; costs), to provide a constant check on actual performance against expected performance.

Subjective evaluation

If we accept that client satisfaction derives largely from perceived effectiveness, it is necessary to find out about client perceptions, and the most obvious method of doing so is to ask!

The subjective questionnaire in Appendix 4 was developed as a complementary tool, to be used in conjunction with the objective checklist. It comprises open-ended, non-directive questions, which seek to elicit the precise opinions/feelings of the client. A more specific form of questionnaire used alone could not achieve this; in imposing a framework on the client, it might completely fail to identify what are, for him, the most salient issues. The questionnaire is a tool by which to assess the client's level of satisfaction at any point in time – as it were, taking the temperature of the water. It provides information which can be acted upon immediately.

To monitor the evaluation process in this way is similar to the internal audit process – a monitoring of the control process. As such, it is desirable organisational practice.

This questionnaire, together with the checklist, can be used as frequently as is thought necessary – half yearly, quarterly or monthly. The optimal frequency depends upon a number of factors; for example, length of contract or size of fee income. It can be used with one or more key people in the client organisation, perhaps at different levels; for example, the chief executive, the marketing manager and the marketing executive with responsibility for PR activities.

A significant problem which must be recognised is that these key people do not remain constant, and are replaced by new individuals with their own perceptions. The questionnaire might usefully be used shortly after a new key executive joins the client organisation.

Research has shown that as the relationship between consultant and client develops over time, so too does the level of tact used in that relationship. The client finds it increasingly difficult and ultimately impossible to confront the consultant with his dissatisfaction, they are too friendly! In the end the client can only cope with this situation by terminating the relationship abruptly. There are two possible solutions to this:

(a)   the consultant and client talk out the problems in an extended interview lasting several hours, after which time tactful conventions can hopefully be overcome; or

(b)   the use of a third party intermediate.

Once the client's perceptions are known, and an objective evaluation of the effectiveness of the relationship has been made, suggestions for improvement should of course be made in close consultation with the client.

The same strictures apply to initial proposal presentation. A participative development of the brief solves many problems which would otherwise arise later on, were the consultant's preferences simply to be imposed without consideration upon the client.

Activity records

Appendix 4 sets out a suggested format for an activity record. This provides basic data to help the evaluation process.

A similar reporting format is often used for costs/expenses.

The problem in implementing this kind of system is that form-filling is always an irksome task. For this reason 'Activity Record' is preferable to, for example, 'Time Sheet'.

Such a system cannot be successfully used unless it is participative; that is, all those involved understand and accept the benefits. The system must also be effectively monitored; for example, directors must ensure that accurate records are being properly kept. Keeping an accurate record of the deployment of human resources is becoming increasingly important, as their value increases. A large sweets manufacturer recently asked its travelling salesmen, over a period of six months, to record their activities at every half hour, the objective being to discover exactly how they spent their time.

The specimen form in Appendix 4 can be used in various ways:

1. The sheets can be filled in as an on-going activity, simply ticking across the page as each activity takes place, or they can be completed retrospectively, eg daily or weekly. The former method is more reliable.

2. Each day records 30 incidents. Research shows this to be sufficient for most executives. The numbers in the lefthand margin denote each separate incident.

3. The list of headings given in this specimen form is exhaustive. One could select only those which appear to be most appropriate and useful.

4. A sensible approach might be to conduct a small pilot study, using the specimen activity record for a brief period, after which it could be reviewed and modified on the basis of experience. Such an experimental period would also yield extremely valuable data about the deployment of resources within the organisation.

5. It is recommended that senior executives should keep this record themselves for an initial period – say one week – to gauge whether it is (a) feasible and (b) useful.

Chapter 6

Success and Failure in PR

As has been seen in earlier chapters, some personality types are simply not suited to the demands of public relations, while others seem to have a natural flair for the work – be it attributable to their empathetic qualities, interest in people, positive attitudes or 'butterfly minds', or, indeed, to a combination of all of these qualities. Conversely, the work of the most brilliantly talented person will be seriously impaired by lack of organisation. Good basic organisation cannot remove the problems caused by sudden eruptions in the workload or by mini-crises, but it provides a framework for coping with the routine, so that sudden problems can be better handled. Sound organisation may be very attractive to potential clients and it helps the establishment of a new account without detracting from existing work.

There are special problems inherent in public relations. The delicate relationships between the individual and the organisation, between one client and another, between systems control and creative innovation, between overreacting and underreacting. In essence, the key to successful and effective public relations lies precisely in getting these balances just right. It is all a question of judgement. To put this another way, one can make a comprehensive list of conditions which are necessary to good public relations, but these conditions would never be sufficient to guarantee success, unless the balance was right.

This statement has important and far-reaching implications for the education and training of public relations practitioners. For while formal education and training, whether academic or practical 'on-the-job' may aim to inculcate a proper understanding and appreciation of the conditions required for successful

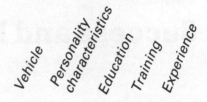

Criterion

Empathy

Organisation

Creativity

Intellect

A grasshopper mind

Motivation

Achievement orientation

General management skills

Stubbornness

Gut instinct

Flair

Rationality

Objectivity

Communication skills

Commitment

Honesty

Perception

Decisiveness

Open-mindedness

Maturity

Balance

Contacts

Optimism

Entrepreneurial flair

Figure 14
**The ideal PR person: checklist of key qualities to be used in staff
selection**

PR, such methods of teaching cannot ensure that the student develops the necessary judgement and sensitivity. This is really a question of learning to learn, which can only be done through experience – although, of course, that experience may be distilled, simulated and, to some extent, accelerated.

LEARNING TO LEARN

The simplest type of system is closed and mechanical. Imagine the workings of a thermostat. The temperature gauge is set at 70°F. During the evening, the actual room temperature falls below this level. An automatic feedback process operates, igniting the heat source until the temperature of 70°F is once again reached.

All social systems differ from this model in that they have the ability to adapt to changes. They are not only able to learn to do or to be something different in order to fit in and cope with their changed surroundings, but ultimately they can learn to learn.

For example, an organisation may learn, through the use of external consultants, to change to a divisionalised or matrix company structure. Such a structure may be more appropriate to the new environmental conditions in which it is operating. However, operating conditions may, of course, change again, either reverting to previous patterns or moving on to something new altogether. In this case, the organisation may need once again to call in the external consultants for advice on how to adapt its structure. Alternatively, the organisation may be more sophisticated and have learned to learn. In which case it may be able to analyse the new situation and, without precedent, devise a completely new solution.

The same principles apply to both the group and the individual. An individual can readily be taught that, for Problem A, he must implement Solution A; when facing Problem B, he must implement Solution B. But what is he to do when Problem C appears – which might be similar to A, similar to B, a combination of factors common to both A and B, or nothing to do with either of them? It is his ability to learn to learn which will determine whether or not he is capable of formulating Solution C.

To put this in a public relations context, a particular campaign or strategy may have proven successful in particular circumstances, but cannot be applied to new situations with any guarantee of success. The key to PR success is the ability to analyse the new situation, draw comparisons with previous situations, identify any common factors, illuminate any significant differences and, using considerable creative as well as analytic and diagnostic skill, devise an appropriate and hence successful solution.

To pursue the analogy with the thermostat, social systems (organisations, groups, human individuals) have the ability to modify the goal itself; to decide to set the regulator at a lower temperature. So, for example, the PR solution, rather than being seen in terms of the effectiveness of regulators (the conventional solution) may be reoriented in terms of energy conservation (the new, original solution).

This is where the creative element of PR can clearly be seen. Advertising may be more creative in an obvious way, but public relations is more a craft than an art. The need for, and opportunities to exploit, lateral thinking are just as real. In fact, lateral thinking is arguably the key ingredient for ensuring continuing success in the public relations field, and it certainly features in many famous PR campaigns.

TEACHING PEOPLE TO LEARN TO LEARN

Experience is the only effective vehicle for learning the art of judgement. Experience can, however, be communicated and it can be distilled. Case studies are one medium for doing this in formal training.

But undoubtedly the best way to learn to learn is through real experiences, and a growing – though by no means universal – trend among PR practitioners is to try and consciously use experiences as a learning device. The PRCA have produced some case material and CAM lecturers are doing likewise.

For an experience to be used effectively as a valuable learning opportunity, the right climate must exist within the group or organisation. Control and appraisal schemes are specially designed to help learning and to improve and modify behaviour; when a problem arises, its causes can be discussed with all concerned, so that a repetition is avoided. However, control and appraisal schemes frequently neglect the use of positive rewards and inducements, and rely solely on negative punishments. As a result, risk taking and innovation are discouraged. People prefer to play safe and avoid the risk of being punished, rather than to be innovative and hope for reward. So it is no use trying to 'set up' experiences as vehicles for individual and organisational learning unless the climate is right. It is important to accept and reward good ideas and intentions, even if these are not immediately successful in implementation. Individuals must feel confident enough to expose their mistakes, so that they and others can learn from them.

> We get in and we talk about it . . . meetings every two to three weeks. We keep ourselves updated. Perhaps we will take a particular topic, like an audio visual. How successful was it? How many people are asking to see it? How many have seen it once?

> One of the things that came up in the Inquiry was that 16 people had seen a fan sparking. Only two people really had any responsibility and action was taken to ascertain why they had not taken their responsibilities. The very fact is that 16 people saw it. We have over the long term to get a situation where any one of the 16 would have said: 'Christ, that fan is sparking. . . .' and done something about it.

Chapter 7
Crisis Situations

Crises such as Chernobyl, Three Mile Island or Seveso, air disasters, oil rig blow outs, or even critical strike threats clearly pose special problems in terms of public relations, as do political crises for companies as well as governments. Is it possible to draw any lessons from the successful handling of public relations in such situations which would be useful in other, more normal, situations? The answer is that certain characteristics of crisis are reflected in a wide range of situations, and there are therefore some extremely valuable lessons to be drawn.

Crises provide an interesting context within which to study any kind of organisation process, since behaviour is usually thrown into relief. Extremes can become the norm.

Crises constitute a very real problem in a large number of business and non-profit making concerns. But the literature of management science has to a large extent neglected the subject.

Hermann provided a set of three dimensions with which to define crisis, and this gives us a useful starting point. A crisis:

(a) threatens high priority values of the organisation;

(b) presents a restricted amount of time in which a response can be made;

(c) is unexpected or unanticipated by the organisation.

The degree to which each of these descriptions applies varies between different types of crisis. It can also be said that a crisis may develop in response to a change of some kind in the operating environment, or it may be internally generated (see Figure 15).

	Internally generated	Caused by a change in the environment
Threatens high priority values of the organisation		
Presents a restricted amount of time in which a response can be made		
Unexpected or unanticipated by the organisation		

Figure 15
Checklist of types of crisis

REACTIONS TO CRISIS

One of the most interesting research findings is that, when facing a crisis situation, managers may react in very restrictive ways. Unfortunately, such behaviour may not prove to be in the best interests of the organisation. When facing a financial crisis, for instance, many managers tighten up control systems and increase the frequency of reporting procedures. However, such behaviour results in the loss or filtering of vital information about what is going on outside the organisation, to which it should be responding.

The critical balance, which is so difficult to achieve, is to ensure a full appreciation of the realities of the situation and its potential seriousness, and to respond in a calm and rational way; and not to panic.

The public relations function is of paramount importance in a crisis. It provides the interpretation of events to which everyone, inside and outside the organisation concerned, will react. In other words, the PR people are influencing, maybe even shaping, other people's perceptions and hence responses.

Most of the experienced PR practitioners interviewed for this book have emphasised that one of the keys to effective public relations is knowing when to react and when not to. They believe that overreacting can do more damage than leaving the thing alone. Quoting Lord Robens, the PR head of one of the nationalised industries explained his own philosophy: 'Today's newspapers, after all, are only tomorrow's fish and chip wrapping.' He maintains that that is a healthy attitude to the press:

> If you worry too much about the press and about what they are saying about you, in a nationalised industry like this, you would never sleep at night. You would never sleep.

However, he also thinks that this is one of the most difficult things to teach new staff, and probably can only be acquired through experience. As a simple operating rule, he advises:

> I think on balance if you are in doubt you should not respond. At least not respond directly, but try and find some other way of making a point or get somebody else to make the point for you.

Indeed, the PR chief of another nationalised industry, who recently moved into the PR function from marketing responsibilities within the same organisation, agrees on the importance of knowing when to react, but says:

> That is something which I certainly have not fully learned yet, and I have to feel my way along this; but I get good advice from my staff on this.

PREDICTABLE AND UNPREDICTABLE CRISES

One of the dimensions useful in defining a crisis concerns the question of whether it was unexpected or unanticipated by the organisation. One has to identify, first, the processes through which the organisation becomes aware of the problem or crisis, and, second, the processes through which it responds and adapts to the need for change. The difference between these processes is critically important, since it distinguishes those crises which are totally unanticipated from those crises which, although privately recognised as being imminent, are not for some time either publicly acknowledged or proactively managed. It seems necessary to include the latter within any definition of crisis in the context of business organisations, since it is not an unusual phenomenon. Indeed, it has been suggested that imminent crises are often apparent within the organisation for up to 12 months – this being the period for disclosing financial data – before being accepted and publicly announced.

In an organisation there are obvious reasons for such reticence. In the case of the individual, this kind of behaviour can be explained in terms of psychological stress: feelings of anxiety and insecurity lead, ultimately, to the withdrawal syndrome.

The banking industry provides an excellent example of the importance of PR. The whole system is based on confidence and trust, and the role of the PR man is to keep those in the best possible condition. This role extends through the whole process, from realisation of the crisis, to acceptance of it, and then to guiding and projecting the organisation's response. It is not too ambitious to suggest that PR might well develop as a discipline to the point where it is helping to analyse the organisation, and to identify possible problem areas and so avert potential crises from developing.

Figure 16 gives a wider working definition of crisis which provided the theme for the advertisement reproduced in Figure 17.

The organisation is:

	RESPONDING	NOT RESPONDING
The organisation is:		
AWARE	1	2
NOT AWARE	4	3

1 – Aware and responding
2 – Aware but not responding
3 – Neither aware nor responding
4 – Not aware but responding nevertheless (?)

Figure 16
Predictable and unpredictable crises

It can be argued that public relations has a role to play in risk management. Calculated risks in statistical terms are not possible, since a risk is a risk and cannot be controlled by measurement. Nevertheless, management must organise to be in a position to cope effectively with crises, or emergency situations, whether predicted or unpredicted, accepted or ignored.

EXAMPLES OF THE PR ROLE IN CRISIS SITUATIONS

The critical question in crisis situations is always how much information should be given.

> Our role is to get authoritative information out as quickly as possible. Our problem is that the management and the people who know the facts are so busy trying to organise a rescue, but we know that if we do not give positive, on the spot information as quickly as possible, the press would go and get it from Charlie's cousin who works in a greengrocer's shop or something like that . . . and it will become garbled and perhaps more horrific than it need be. So we have somehow to try and persuade management to brief the press quickly and authoritatively.

Similarly:

> I think we have an obligation to tell the public the facts in non-emotive terms. Not to conceal things, because there is the argument that if you tell them too much you frighten them, there is also the argument that if you do not tell them anything you frighten them even more. And our job is to see that the facts are not distorted, and if you try to withhold them the distortion sets in.

Contingency planning

A broad range of potential crises and disaster situations are in fact covered by the elaborate contingency plans.

> There is, for example, for every electricity authority or generating authority a crisis plan for dealing with a nuclear alert. But it has never been used, because actually power stations are incredibly safe.

There was one crisis where a power station looked as if it might blow up and scatter the area around with coal dust. But it did not happen. At the end of the day I suppose you could say we alerted people unnecessarily.

Contingency planning depends upon a rigorously logical consideration of all possible events and, with added complexity, all possible combinations of events and their consequences. Most contingency plans are never put to the test, of course, though there are practical exceptions:

Unfortunately, there have been far too many of these incidents in the past, and so we have a certain amount of experience, and we have worked out a certain amount of drill.

Emergency organisation

All of the people who are directly responsible for handling the public relations function in a crisis or emergency situation, describe contingency plans which establish very similar organisations to cope with the immediate problems. In every case the PR chief remains in London, sending a senior person to the site as quickly as possible. Where necessary, he is assisted by people co-opted in from other areas near to the site. All emphasise the importance of this spokesman being able to speak with authority; he has to have some 'clout', he has to 'be able to boss the press as well . . . to stop the press getting in the way of the rescue operation'. This is recognised as a difficult job for the man on the spot, and invariably he will have undergone intensive television training.

The PR chief is usually responsible for coordination.

The chap on the spot is having briefing sessions, press conferences, arranging interviews for television, that sort of thing, but he never sees what comes out. So one of my functions is to keep an eye on the box and radio and tell him what has been said and if something has been said which is misleading or damaging, to try and put it right.

. . . we agree a brief, and this is all linked up to London with radio communications.

We have to avoid using the services that are going to be needed for the rescue operation, for example, telephones, things like that.

We have video equipment so that all television programmes, and radio programmes, are monitored and we have our own VTRs of them, so we know exactly what was said and what was done and we can get a consistent line. We have land line conference facilities, so we are in constant contact, so the whole thing is geared up on a fairly sophisticated basis.

The critical coordinating role of the PR chief is recognised explicitly in many organisations. Often, for example, under emergency conditions, he is able to specify what resources must be allocated to cope with the situation; he advises the chief executive about resource allocation. It is often indeed the PR department which receives information about the crisis before the rest of the management hierarchy, since

the press and news agencies are in business to get information quickly, are they not? And so quite often we get a call from maybe a local agency man who has been tipped off that ambulances have been called to a certain site.

Within that particular organisation, this informal channel of communication has been recognised officially, so that while during working hours the normal hierarchical communication structure operates, outside office hours the official line of communication is through the PR department.

Lessons to be learned

The military model is still used for organisation efficiency. Under conditions of extreme danger inefficiencies will tend to be minimised. Certain lessons do appear from what has been said about the establishing of emergency organisations: clear lines of communication, coordination to achieve consistency of information, the risks of misinformation filling any vacuums.

Several people comment on the relationship between the PR team and the press and other media, during crises. The PR man on the spot necessarily has a special role to play and a special relationship with the press; he has to 'boss' the media; in other words, his relationship is probably more effective.

I think that the heat of the moment often engenders a greater degree of understanding between the media and us . . . a much greater level of understanding and co-operation. It is a much healthier situation in fact than you get generally speaking with a serious TV programme, like 'World in Action' or 'Panorama', because they may have been motivated by some pressure group. Now in an incident situation something has actually happened, men are dead, for instance. There is less chance of dishonesty, there is a much greater relationship. We have had a couple of rough deals . . . but never on incidents, only on issues.

Chapter 8

To Grow or Not to Grow: the Dilemma of the PR Consultancy

In any profit making PR operation, cash flow management must extend to the planning of new business. New accounts need to be brought on line as existing business is completed or threatens to dry up. Clearly this is more than a simple process of budgetary control.

Beyond the question of immediate survival lies the issue of growth. Is there an optimal size for a PR operation, or indeed for any other kind of entrepreneurial organisation? Most PR companies are small but this leads to problems such as deciding where best to channel profits. On the other hand, companies which decide to go for growth, and to overcome any inherent constraints on growth which exist, face the following questions:

- how to find new business
- how best to fit new business into the existing organisation structure
- how to keep new business.

THE GROWTH PATTERN OF ORGANISATIONS

There are three stages of corporate development:

- pioneering
- specialisation
- integration.

The transition from the pioneering stage to specialisation is particularly problematic, for this marks the critical turning point in the career of the entrepreneur: the point at which he must decide either to stand still (which strategy may in fact prove impossible) or to opt for continued development, which requires organisation.

The essential functions for any organisation are:

- maintenance
- adaptation
- goal attainment
- integration.

Where one or more of these is not met, an organisation is unlikely to survive on its own. The successful entrepreneur manages all four functions himself, until he opts for company growth. The key problems typically facing the entrepreneur at this stage include:

- how to structure the organisation in the face of increasing size – specifically, how to delegate the processes of decision making
- how to structure the organisation so that it is effective at both the routine maintenance and the adaptive functions.

Many entrepreneurs never manage this transition. Hence the proliferation of one-man outfits in public relations. Companies going through the transition from a 'man, a boy and a dog' operation to a larger organisation are very often bedevilled by personnel problems. Frequent and unanticipated changes in personnel create a series of crisis points. The cause of such crises can usually be traced back to one or more of the following:

- inadequate control
- ambiguous roles
- centralised decision making.

Recovery and continued development is often dependent upon the company obtaining larger, more stable accounts, which give greater continuity of personnel, successful delegation of various aspects of the business and improved controls.

Increasing size tends to lead to greater formalisation of roles. This ensures continuity and stability and reduces ambiguity, but at the same time it reduces flexibility and the expression of individual personalities. Hence the tendency for PR agencies to remain small. Regimentation is incompatible with individual responsibility and creative implementation. Similarly, as size increases, so decisions are decentralised. But which decisions to decentralise and to whom?

Very often a major stumbling block – for strong psychological reasons – is the recruiting of an effective number two man to the entrepreneur. In organisation terms, the problem really hinges on the need to differentiate between routine, operational activities, and longer-term, strategic, adaptive thinking and planning, and then the need to integrate the two.

Specialisation versus coordination is, perhaps *the* key problem of organisation design (see Chapter 2), and is never more prominent than at this stage in a company's development. Only if some system such as work groups or teams or 'organisational families' can be made viable, can an organisation at the pioneering stage in its develcpment hope to progress effectively to the integration stage and in so doing bypass the intermediate stage of specialisation.

EVALUATING NEW BUSINESS

Development of the company reaches a point where the successful entrepreneur must be selective in the new business he accepts. There are sound organisation and business reasons, for example, for attracting only compatible types of business and developing a clearly visible distinctive competence in specific areas, quite apart from the obvious risks of taking on business which is bad from a financial or image point of view.

Following are some suggested criteria for the evaluation of new business opportunities and new business proposals.

They are not intended to be comprehensive, but should provide a useful basis for discussion and elaboration.

Clearly some criteria will be given greater importance than others. The problem is how to compile an overall assessment using these criteria as a framework.

Distinctive competence

The first problem is to define the distinctive competence of the company or PR department. Does this relate to the way in which it runs campaigns? Or to dealing with specific types of business/industry?

New business opportunities can be evaluated using the following questions:

1. Is the distinctive competence appropriate for the new business?

2. Is the new business complementary to existing business? If not, does the necessary diversification follow in a logical direction for it, and one that could lead to further business in the new area?

3. Will the new business enhance or weaken corporate image?

4. Is the company/department currently organised to be able to take on the new business effectively, without risk to existing business, within the time scale envisaged?

5. Is it probable that the new business will satisfy its profitability requirement (eg 20 per cent)?
    Note: a minimum fee could be established (eg £20,000 pa), below which the potential profitability of the new business (ie level of return as compared with level of resource input) would be very carefully scrutinised.

6. Is there a possibility of the new business creating further new business opportunities, eg a one-off assignment leading to an on-going relationship; work for one company leading to relationships with other associated, subsidiary or parent companies?

7. What is the growth potential of the specific new business opportunity? What factors will affect the development of this potential, and to what extent can changes in those factors be forecast?

8. What is the possibility of the client delaying/defaulting in payments to the company?

9. What is the reason for the new business opportunity presenting itself?

Why does the client want to retain the company? Is this acceptable to the company?

Evaluating acceptable proposals

While it is probably not necessary, or even desirable, to stipulate a uniform formula for new business proposals, it is useful to draw up a checklist of criteria for evaluating acceptable proposals. A clearly recognisable house style also helps the professional appearance of proposals.

Such a list of criteria for evaluation might include the following:

1. Format. The proposal should have a logical structure which is clearly set out on the contents page. It should be concise, lucid and generally well written. A well spaced layout not only improves the appearance of the document but also facilitates ease and speed of reading; appropriate emphases and the flow of the argument are also more obvious. When used selectively, statistics can indicate a good research input. Detailed statistics, presented as clearly as possible, are best relegated to an appendix. Where it is necessary to introduce some figures into the text, these are most easily interpreted if presented in diagrammatic or graphical form.

2. A good proposal should state specifically:

    (a) The objectives of the proposed PR activity. These stated objectives should seek to answer the following questions:
    - What is the message to be communicated?
    - To whom is this message to be communicated?
    - How is this message to be communicated?
    - What will happen as a result of this message being communicated and received by this audience?

    (b) The methods which will be used to achieve those objectives.

    (c) The deployment of resources – time input, financial resources etc. Specifically, how resources will be allocated to
    - client liaison
    - press liaison
    - special events
    - planning

- reporting
- miscellaneous.

(d) The methods used by the company or department to evaluate and review on-going PR activity.

3. Except in special cases (eg renewal or expansion of existing business) it may be useful to argue generally for the role of PR, and specifically to demonstrate the relevance and potential benefit to the client company of PR activity. The proposal might include some brief comment on the effectiveness of external PR agencies as compared with in-house PR departments.

4. A professional proposal should also indicate, if not demonstrate, a knowledge of the client's industry and of his particular organisation. If possible, it should illustrate how PR activity could help solve some key problems currently facing the client.

5. Some indication of the company or PR department's distinctive competence should be given. In which ways is it a preferable alternative to other PR companies which might be submitting competitive proposals?

6. It is important from the point of view of credibility to give potential clients a clear indication of (a) the current portfolio of clients with, if appropriate, renewal rates, and (b) the organisation and flexibility of available resources within the company. It is a debatable point whether it is best to include this information in the proposal itself, or as some kind of attached prospectus. The best strategy tends to vary according to the individual case.

CASE STUDY

The best way of understanding the problems involved in fitting new business into an existing organisation structure is to use a specific example. We consider here how PR Consultants Ltd prepared itself to receive prospective new business accounts.

Two points were established at the outset as being crucial to the search for a solution:

1. Any modification of the existing organisation structure must be made with an awareness of the processes involved. The structure should make easier the smooth running of the company.

2. Certain basic assumptions had to be questioned and challenged, and not be automatically incorporated in new structure proposals.

PRC Ltd's existing organisation structure

The structure of the organisation before any changes were made is illustrated in Figure 18. The first stage in looking at the possibilities of reorganisation was a role analysis exercise. The usefulness of this exercise was that by focussing on each individual's role within the organisation, it related structure and process and highlighted any mismatch between the two. Focussing on the dynamic aspects of the organisation's activities, this approach also identified those basic assumptions which needed to be questioned. This approach reflected a personal and professional disaffection with the imposed package solutions favoured by many of the larger management consulting firms.

Three problem areas were identified:

1. *The role of Number Two to the Chairman*

   The Number Two's role appeared to be perceived, both by himself and by the Chairman, as that of (a) Managing Director Elect and (b) Manager of Group A. Role (a) would imply some kind of authority over the other directors, but as yet this relationship appeared ambiguous, and some future conflict was inevitable. Overt (as opposed to covert) conflict had so far been avoided simply because there had been no need for the two groups to coordinate in any way.

   Current proposals seemed to mean that Number Two would be displaced by a new Group Managing Director who might be less able to cope with that role. The question to be asked here was whether the founder would really prefer to limit his own role to that of Chairman, or whether he envisaged developing his role more as that of Chief Executive.

2. *Bases for divisional split*

The company was divided, according to type of client, into Consumer and Industrial accounts and Commercial accounts. The basic assumption to be questioned here concerned the criteria used to split the company in this way. Do the different types of activity require distinctive competences? If so, is it logical to structure the organisation on this basis? Or is this distinction artificial? Would it be more logical to divide the company on the basis of clients/accounts?

The existing intention to place new consumer business under the aegis of the Industrial and Commercial group would have led to an organisation structure divided on the basis of type of activity and client/account. This would have been ambiguous and confusing. Consider, for example, the position of X in Figure 19: to whom should he be responsible?

The acquisition of significant business which blurred the traditional divide emphasised the urgent need to define the criteria to be used in structuring the organisation.

3. *Integration*

Role relations showed a hierarchical structure. Most importantly, there appeared to be virtually no cross-functional communication at any level, from the directors downwards, although vertical relationships and communications appeared to be satisfactory. This communications pattern had probably developed because previously all members of the staff had related to the Chairman/Managing Director on a one-to-one basis. The need for lateral communications was becoming increasingly important as, for example, the X account and the Y account failed to fall neatly within the existing divisions of the organisation. Integration would also help generate new business from existing accounts.

Who should perform this integrating function? Should coordination be channelled through the Chairman/Managing Director? Through the Group Managing Directors? Or through their staff?

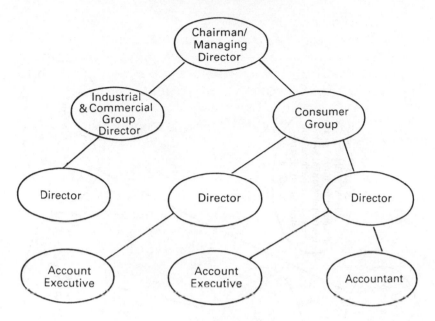

Figure 18
PRC Ltd's existing organisation structure

Drawbacks of the existing structure of PRC Ltd

At the level of the Management Committee, lateral communications appeared to be weak, and as a result the role of the Committee appeared limited. There were a number of possible explanations for this, for example:

(a) highly centralised control by the Chairman/Managing Director;

(b) lack of appreciation of the need for lateral communications;

(c) too little time because of high work pressure.

The terms of reference for the Management Committee probably also needed to be amplified.

There was also a need for improved communication and coordination mechanisms at all levels in the organisation below the Management Committee.

105

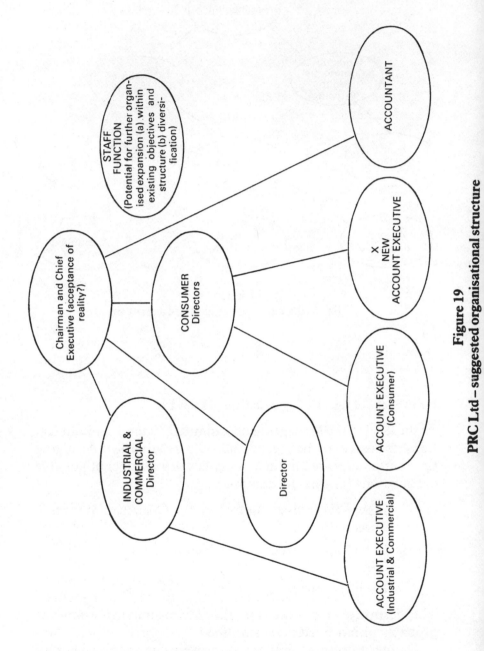

Figure 19
PRC Ltd – suggested organisational structure

Proposed reorganisation of PRC Ltd

The new structure which was proposed is illustrated in Figure
19. Although one of several directors reporting directly to the
Chairman/Managing Director, the Number Two would be
primus inter pares, deputising where necessary. Other Groups
would, however, work laterally with the Number Two.

This structure would facilitate further organised expansion
within the usual range of activities, or the diversifying of the
company into consultancy activities. It also offered the possibility of setting up separate staff functions; for example, finance
and accounting, personnel, and administration, if the company
continued to grow to a point at which separation of line and staff
seemed preferable.

The new structure would put the company in a position to
exploit new business opportunities which arose as a result of
work in one Group, but which offered future work within the
scope of another Group.

A number of recommendations were made:

1. The development of more lateral processes at all levels
    within the company; improved horizontal communica-
    tion and coordination. For example: improve the effec-
    tiveness of management meetings and amplify their
    terms of reference; use of information exchanges be-
    tween Groups; suggested areas of possible cooperation.

2. Where a specific account falls into more than one Group
    or does not fall logically into any of them, a possible
    solution would be to elect a project coordinator on an ad
    hoc basis. Such an arrangement allows far greater
    flexibility than the establishing of an elaborate matrix or
    project organisation, though maintaining the balance
    between flexibility and ambiguity remains a very com-
    plex task.

3. Task forces could be set up to process new business
    propositions. A task force is temporarily superimposed
    on the functional structure, and is used to short-circuit
    communication lines in times of high uncertainty. When
    the uncertainty decreases, the functional hierarchy
    resumes its guiding influence.
    Such task forces have the following advantages:

(a) they increase flexibility;

(b) they are temporary, and are dissolved as soon as the problem or task is solved;

(c) they give increased responsibility to individuals without a concomitant and necessarily permanent increase in status;

(d) problems are removed from higher levels in the hierarchy and can be solved at quite low levels in the organisation.

They only work, however, if people behave in a confronting, problem-solving manner.

4. Increase in scope the role of staff personnel. Specifically, increase centralisation of the financial control function. This would:

(a) facilitate greater control over profitability;

(b) provide a much needed integrative function between the various groups within the company, enabling it to function more as a cohesive organisation. The integrator role, to be effective, must have credibility with all groups in the company and be seen to be unbiased. The effectiveness of this role is increased by the amount of supporting factual information available; for example, an information system reporting actual expenditures against functional or departmental budgets. This role is in fact very difficult; it is suggested that it would initially require the overt support of the Chairman/ Managing Director to give it credibility.

This is not to suggest that the autonomy of the various group managers should be reduced with regard to financial planning and control within their own group budgets. But, as a profit centre, each group would operate within a better defined and centrally controlled framework of financial objectives.

5. Encourage more active role negotiation, specifically between (a) the Chairman/Managing Director and other company directors, and (b) directors managing separate

groups within the company. The point here is that the ambiguity and potential conflict must be resolved on a lateral basis; ie, an appeal to higher authority is unsatisfactory in that this leaves unresolved the basic points of contention. It is infinitely preferable for such negotiation to be carried out in an open, honest manner. This increases the general level of trust within an organisation.

6.   Exposure of key personnel to current thinking in the area of organisational behaviour. It is suggested that this is most profitable if the learning experience is shared with other members of the role set or work group.

RECENT DEVELOPMENTS

During the past decade, the PR industry has grown at a phenomenal pace. In 1986 the *Economist* reported that the industry had grown at the rate of 48 per cent, making it the fastest-growing sector of the UK economy. Since then the growth has been steadying at approximately 25 per cent each year. During this period, the publicly quoted PR conglomerate has emerged to dominate the PR business. The rise and fall of some of these companies has highlighted the weakness of the management function in many of these fast-growing organisations.

At the start of this period of dynamic change a number of companies vied for top position. The Good Relations Group plc was the first to seek and obtain a full listing on the Stock Exchange in 1983. It was the largest PR organisation in the UK between 1982 and 1986. It aimed to challenge the supremacy of Hill and Knowlton (the subsidiary of J Walter Thompson) and Burson Marsteller as the world's largest. In 1984 the Good Relations Group was at its peak with anticipated profits of £1.3m for that year. But on 23 December 1984 an article in the *Sunday Telegraph* (headlined 'Poor Relations') reported on the rumour that the company planned to close their recently opened City office. The City editor forecast that this would lead to the loss of staff and clients. The following day the shares, then standing at an all time high of 280, fell 100p; a Stock Exchange record fall for one day. On 30 August 1985, seven months later, Maureen Smith, the Chief Executive and architect of Good Relations' growth, left the company. The well-publicised difficulties both before and after her departure have highlighted the volatility of the PR service business.

Between 1986 and 1989 the Shandwick Group became the largest independent company in the world. In 1989 the leading companies, according to PRCA, were as follows:

Leading PR companies in the UK over £4m in PR fee income

> Shandwick
> Charles Barker
> Burson Marsteller
> Dewe Rogerson
> The Grayling Company
> Hill & Knowlton
> Valin Pollen
> Broad St
> Countrywide
> Good Relations
> D J Edleman
> Kingsway Rowland
> Paragon Communications

All recorded growth organically and by acquisition. The growth of the PR industry continues apace at a compound figure of 25 per cent. Colin Thompson, Director of PRCA, has remarked on this growth having taken place despite the problems of inadequate staff training and management expertise. 'The industry has started to import management and the general standards are now improving from the days of the cottage industry.'

The two biggest problems facing the PR industry at the present time are the lack of effective management and of training. The dearth of managers and well-trained executives has inhibited the growth of consultancies and undermined the stability of many established companies. The demand for PR specialists has made PR head-hunting a new opportunity for the recruitment businesses.

Inevitably highly publicised defections of key personnel put increasing demands on the management structures of the newly emerging publicly quoted companies.

One of the weakest features of the public relations business is the lack of management skills in running the companies themselves. On 6 January 1987 the *Financial Times* reported:

To Grow or Not to Grow

Ten directors quit PR company – the resignations yesterday of 10 directors of one of Britain's fastest-growing leading public relations companies stem from serious boardroom differences that seem to be symptoms of a deeper malaise affecting the PR industry as a whole.

There is nothing new in the 'deeper malaise affecting the PR industry as a whole' as reported by David Churchill of the *Financial Times*. It stems from the fact that the buccaneering individuals who initially succeed in establishing successful PR consultancies have little or no experience of the management requirements for running a large company. In most cases the structures they establish are inappropriate to the 'task culture' requirements of the PR function. Inevitably as the structures become overloaded and bureaucratic they cease to function.

Can the new style PR publicly quoted companies continue to grow or will there be further break-ups and collapses, as characterised by the past experiences of Good Relations, the Moorgate Group and the much publicised problems of companies like Charles Barker, Streets and Broad Street?

On a small scale, the industry is facing the problems of growth that have fuelled the management debate about the multinational conglomerates. Professor Michael Porter of the Harvard Business School, author of *Competitive Strategy* and *Competitive Advantage* focuses on the practical choices open to businesses in building the web of strategic alliances they need and highlights the role that the PR practitioner can play in the new era of multinational organisations. What is clear is that the PR quoted companies will only be able to maintain their status as growth companies by using their 'paper' to acquire more companies. But the lessons that have been learnt from recent experience in the PR 'people' business, is that the organisation will only remain intact if the operating companies retain their original ecologies. Centralisation of functions like accounts or exercising central control over management decisions will lead to disenchantment and continuing breakaways. The organismic flair of the 'task culture' will not be maintained by changing the cultures.

This lesson probably lay at the heart of the early success of the Saatchi & Saatchi Group. However, the decline of profits after ten years' continuous growth in 1989 has highlighted Saatchi's difficulty in maintaining the 'task cultures' in their worldwide business.

A similar philosophy lies behind the extraordinary growth of the WPP Group led by Martin Sorrell, former finance director of Saatchi & Saatchi. In 1989, after less than three years, WPP became the second largest international marketing services group with the acquisition of Ogilvy & Mather, which joined J Walter Thompson, and an impressive range of other acquisitions.

WPP have adopted as a basic tenet of their business philosophy that each acquisition must remain independent and continue to operate in the market niche it has established. The founders and existing management teams are motivated by further tranches of 'buy-out' cash if they grow by 20 per cent per annum and maintain a 20 per cent profit margin. Their executives are given incentives in the form of share options and profit sharing. The culture that has brought the company its early success is maintained through 'non-interference' clauses in the acquistion agreement. The 'task culture' therefore appears to remain as strong within the federation of the WPP Group as in its earlier independent state.

The public relations industry in the late 1980s and early 1990s is likely to grow at between 20 and 30 per cent per annum. A new generation of consultancies is already developing with special niche markets as their spearhead to market growth.

The completion of the internal market in 1992 will also present a further important new dimension for public relations practices. Specialist agencies able to operate across European countries will be attractive to multi-national organisations. There will be a continuing growth of specialist consultancies, particularly in the areas of Strategic Positioning, Public Affairs, and Issue, Crisis & Events Management.

Another important development which took place in 1987 has probably affected the attitudes of the PR directors of the larger consultancies. This is that under the terms of the new Companies Act, directors of companies are personally liable for any debts incurred by the company should it fail. This is a new and onerous responsibility and for directors of PR companies which have not matured or developed a proper financial information system, could be a source of considerable concern. It could also provide a further incentive for breakaways from the large companies.

Chapter 9

In-house PR or External Agency?

The issue of whether to use an external public relations consultancy or an internal department has become increasingly relevant. Many organisations are cutting down on internal staff and PR departments are always a target. But the question is often tinged with emotion, and the arguments, on both sides, are often rather more rationalisations than reasons.

In general terms, public relations is the same kind of activity, be it practised by an internal department or an outside concern. There are, nevertheless, significant differences, and these provide arguments for and against, depending upon the particular circumstances.

To illustrate: it may be argued that an external agency can provide a higher degree of objectivity; but, against this, an internal department has access to knowledge and experience of the particular company. Outside contracts may be more expensive; but, against this, the client may feel in a politically more powerful position when it comes to evaluating performance, and the result may well prove ultimately more cost effective. An internal department should, in theory, feel in closer contact with the client and his needs; but intra-organisational relationships often tend, ironically, to be weaker or more problematic than relationships with people outside the organisation. In both types of operation there is a basic client relationship, but, again ironically, in an in-house operation roles may be assumed, taken for granted, with little effort given to defining them properly. Consequently, there may well be more problems of role ambiguity and conflict than in situations where relationships have to be established and developed from base.

A general change is taking place in the way external PR agencies and in-house operations are being used. It would not be true to say that there is – or is likely to be – a swing away from external agencies. Rather, the decision is now tending to be made on the basis of a much more sophisticated appreciation of the real and potential role of public relations, which, as was observed in Chapter 1, is a many-sided activity.

External operations and in-house facilities are now being more appropriately used. Specifically, external agencies are increasingly being used in two types of situation:

(a) where specialist expertise is needed, and this is not available in-house;

(b) as a buffer, where the existing in-house resources cannot cope with a temporary crisis or peak in demand and workload.

These are precisely the areas where external operations have a distinctive competitive advantage. Clearly, external agencies should bear this in mind when considering their own business development programmes.

> Because of our limited, very small staff, I use outside support services. I use an outside advertising agency, printers, design people who will help me put together a presentation. And because of my years in Fleet Street, if I do not have the time to write a speech or an article, I can call on a friendly journalist who will do something for me on a freelance basis. So I can run what is a very complicated department with a variety of things because I have those outside services. They are not on contract, they are freelance people whom I will call upon because of their particular specialised abilities.

> I use them both because they are specialists and also to cope with fluctuations.

> Occasionally because the requirement is so specialised that I could not do it without a lot of research, but also when it becomes impossible for me, I cry out and bring them in literally to assist me. But I do not use a full-time public relations consultancy. I do the work that they would do, I do that myself.

The fact that external consultancies charge substantial fees is a frequent objection to their use. But in situations where buffer resources or specialist skills are being bought, the expenditure can be well justified. It has to be seen against the alternatives of making a permanent commitment to cover such situations, or failing to cope when unexpected situations do arise.

> For odd things we do use an external agency – to help cope with pressure – but they are more expensive! Very often valuable, though. I think it is necessary to use them. I think it is a matter of circumstances. I think if you are needing to use public relations not long term, you do not want the commitment of someone, then it is fine and valuable.

> They make different contributions . . . specialist knowledge.

> I think there are times when they are valuable and necessary with work pressures and when they have particular skills which you do not.

There is a further, processual, advantage in using external consultants and this relates back to what was said earlier about the developing and frequently debilitating level of tact in any close working relationship. The outsider brings objectivity to his analysis of the situation, and, equally important, is not barred, psychologically or organisationally, from communicating his analysis and consequent recommendations.

> I think often the value of an outside consultancy is to get an outside view which is not an inside one. People look at it objectively, and they can say harsh things which a chappie who has, after all, got to get his salary at the end of the month, cannot afford to say. I think this is often their value, as devil's advocate.

> We use the external agency as a sounding board as well.

But of course there is another facet to such objectivity.

> Using our own people. I have never dreamt of using consultants. People in the area are going to be affected, and I think have a right to have direct access to the Board and not some consultants.

Particular circumstances will determine which quality is the more critical: objectivity or empathy. Selecting the most appropriate balance between the two is part of the perceptive skill of the public relations specialist. Implementing the right

115

mix is a measure of his organising and managerial ability. This is the art of judgement discussed earlier.

> We believe that MPs, newspapers, certainly would get very testy if they found they were dealing with consultants.

But the best consultants are increasingly accepted even in a direct contact role with these audiences. Overall, there is a growing appreciation of the need for and potential value of public relations activity generally, and of the consultant in particular situations. More and more organisations are reducing their in-house PR operations, as they see the need for well conceived and properly organised public relations activities. PR is no longer seen as something which can reasonably be left to chance, or as a casual adjunct to busy executives' other (primary) concerns.

There is a changing view of the relevance of internal PR departments as opposed to external agencies. In the early 1980s, at a time of cutbacks and recession, there was a trend to disband the internal PR department in favour of the external agency. But increasingly there is a more sophisticated understanding of the importance of both. Internal operations are not being set up in order to replace the external agency. Instead, the resources needed to manage the PR process effectively are being analysed and, where relevant, the internal and external resources are being upgraded and extended. More appropriate uses of the special skills of the external agency are being assessed. The arguments for a more careful analysis and assessment of the precise needs of the PR function are now recognised. For example, specialist assistance provided externally to undertake a comprehensive 'communications audit' will establish the most cost effective way to achieve defined public relations goals.

In the past few years government departments, nationalised and privatised industries and local authorities have begun to undertake large-scale audits of their requirements. But the competition to undertake this management consultancy work has increased dramatically. Accountancy firms, management consultants and corporate design consultants, as well as the PR agencies, have been pitching for this lucrative work.

So the scene is undergoing a radical change and the external versus internal resources debate is being replaced by a new scenario. The big questions being faced by the PR practitioner are how to get the maximum impact from the scarce PR resources of manpower; how to structure the PR process to cover the strategic positioning of the organisation in its environment; how to manage the big issues that will determine growth and survival.

Chapter 10

PR Management Training

There are two ways of changing someone's behaviour. You can either change the way he thinks and behaves or you can change his conditions or circumstances so that he is more likely to behave in the way you want.

Similarly, there are two basic approaches to the problem of improving the effectiveness of the public relations function – whether we are talking about an in-house operation or an outside agency. You can either seek to develop the practitioner himself (management development) or you can work at improving his situation (organisation development).

Combining the two classifications in cube form illustrates the broad range of possibilities for effecting changes with any organisation (see Figure 20). This extends from the use of positive sanctions (rewards) in an attempt to alter a person's intention and hopefully his behaviour, as part of a planned programme of management development (Box A), to the opposite extreme of using negative sanctions (punishments) to seek to alter that person's circumstances so that he is more likely to conform to whatever is required of him, where this is seen as part of an orchestrated attempt to develop the organisation (Box B). Many variations lie in between.

ORGANISATION DEVELOPMENT

The basic problem for all organisations is to resist the inevitable tendency to stagnate. Using the terms introduced in earlier sections, organisations must learn to learn, rather than simply learn; they must be adaptive rather than adapted.

119

STRATEGY

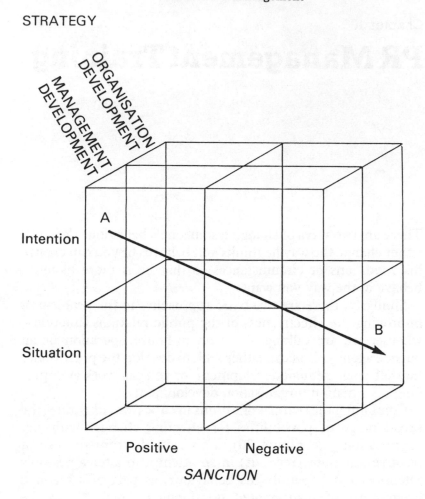

Figure 20
Vehicles for Change

Organisation development (OD) can be characterised as follows:

1. It is an educational strategy designed to bring about planned organisation change. At its most simple, this involves a questionnaire/group discussion exercise. More elaborately, group sensitivity training is used. Efforts at change are usually directed at the intervening variables: values, attitudes, relationships and climates,

rather than at the end-result variables: the organisation's goals, structure and technology. But it is argued by some that more effective and cheaper efforts might instead focus on those other parts of the system.

2. Most OD programmes are generated by some kind of problem, often crisis, facing the organisation. Changes are therefore directly related to their role in solving that particular problem.

3. The educational philosophy of OD programmes builds on past behavioural experiences.

4. Change agents are usually brought in from outside the organisation. This preference is explained not only in terms of objectivity but also by the extra political muscle attaching to an outsider.

5. Change agents and clients must work together to achieve success; Bennis uses the word 'collaborate' with care. This is totally dissimilar from the perceived relationship followed by many conventional management consultants.

6. There is an underlying philosophy among professionals involved in OD programmes, and hence discernible in most OD exercises too. For example, organismic organisations are more humane, democratic and ultimately more efficient than bureaucracies. They are concerned with real, authentic relationships, and so with increasing interpersonal skills.

Essentially, organisation development is about choice, and increasing the range of choice at both the individual and the organisational level, so that better decisions can be made in a rapidly changing world.

Two examples of attempts at organisation development and their implications for effective PR behaviour have been given in earlier chapters. Here are three more brief examples taken from the research.

An American bank
We have been pretty flexible in the past. There have been big changes in the Board itself and it has adapted; there was a big reorganisation in 1967 and minor changes are going on all the time. The structure remains basically the same. The impetus for

change typically comes either from myself or the PROs; they are really the key people. We do all the production work and they are the users; they will quickly tell me if I am not providing them with the right gear.

A local authority

Well, I am in the process at the moment of having certain organisational changes made. One which we are thinking about at the moment, which has not yet been promulgated and which is not necessarily going to take place, but I hope will, is the subject of greater involvement of local authorities. By the Acts of 1972 and 1978 shire counties are having a greater responsibility for the total requirements within their area, and this legislation now means that they are bound to take us into account, whereas hitherto they did not necessarily take account of us. In order to meet this requirement the local shire authorities need to talk to us and need to negotiate with us, and this involves a far greater degree of work and general involvement by local management which hitherto has not been necessary. They need to produce a total integrated scheme for their shire, and you cannot produce a total integrated scheme without us, and on the other hand if they want additional services to the ones that already exist somebody has to pay for them. And the nation will not pay for them through the Department, the shires have to pay for them, so that means negotiations and consultations with these people. Local management has to take on this additional responsibility and burden and one part of this responsibility must be communications and public affairs, and PR. And we need to organise ourselves properly in order to cope with that changing requirement. So perhaps that is an example of where our organisation can and must change, in my judgement, to deal with the problems that are facing us at the present time.

The Health and Safety Executive

In organisational terms I think what we need is just two things. One is the time, the facility to educate inspectors to understand the issues. A lot of the time we are doing it, but it is slow, and this is not surprising because they are hard worked, and we are hard worked, and we do not have time actually to take them to one side in seminars to teach them. I think that will undoubtedly come over the long term. Also relevant to that is the fact that, though they do not realise it, 60 per cent of my branch's function is servicing and 40 per cent is policy making; though these inspectors do not realise it, in a few years' time, just as we service them, they will be servicing us, in execution of PR work. There is that requirement.

The other requirement is a very simple one. It will not happen in my time, I will not try to make it happen in my time, but at some stage the Government machinery has to recognise that the top limit of professionalism has to be raised in my job. Not in me, in my job; in that eventually the status of communications requirement in PR has to be enhanced because of the very nature of the job. It will not happen in my time because I would not bother too much to press for it; it would take a long time and eventually, when I come to retirement, there will be a recognition of it. But at the moment, the Information Class was brought into the Civil Service in 1946 as a result of an investigation. The Crombie Report indicated that there should be people brought in from outside, people with various specialisms. He said that in the Central Office of Information there would be no one above the grade of Principal. So since 1946 the grading has gone up, but it is still a bit below the other administrative grades – well, in fact it is a lot because I do not think we go as far as Grade 6 but I think we get to an Under Secretary level in my area. And I think that will come; and I think that is a greater recognition by management in PR in terms of status. But I am not too worried because it will come of its own accord; it will generate itself.

Those are the only two things.

MANAGEMENT DEVELOPMENT

Figure 21 compares and contrasts the methods and objectives of management development with those of organisation development. It would seem that attempts to develop management potential within public relations are more common than forays into the world of OD. But which is more effective? Should investment in management development, at an exponential or at least increased rate be continued, or should some of these resources be channelled into organisation development exercises?

Before opting for either of these strategies, the roles of various interested parties must be considered: CAM, PRCA, public relations agencies, in-house PR bosses, the chief executives of big business and the nationalised industries, academics, government and the trade unions.

Category	Organisation Development	Management Development
reasons for use	Need to improve overall organisational effectiveness; typical examples of tough problems to be solved: inter-unit conflict; confusion stemming from recent management change; loss of effectiveness due to inefficient organisational structure; lack of teamwork.	Need to improve overall effectiveness of manager; managers do not know company policy or philosophy; managers do not have certain skills; managers seem to be unable to act decisively.
typical goals	To increase the effectiveness of the organisation by: creating a sense of 'ownership' of organisation objectives throughout the workforce; planning and implementing changes more systematically; facilitating more systematic problem solving on the job; to reduce wasted energy and effort by creating conditions where conflict among people is managed openly rather than handled indirectly or unilaterally; to improve the quality of decisions by establishing conditions where	To teach company values and philosophy; to provide practice in management skills which lead to improved organisational effectiveness; to increase ability to plan, coordinate, measure, and control efforts of company units to gain a better understanding of how the company functions to accomplish its goals.

decisions are made on the basis of competence rather than organisational role or status; to integrate the organisation's objectives with the individual's goals by developing a reward system which supports achievement of the organisation's mission as well as individual efforts toward personal development and achievement.

Sending of manager to some educational programme; job rotation of managers; specialised training 'packages';

interventions for producing change

education and problem solving is on the job; learning while problem solving and solving problems while learning following a diagnosis; utilisation of one or more of the following techniques:

team building
training programmes
inter-group confrontations
data feedback
techno-structural
interventions

change in organisational structure
job enrichment
change in physical environment (social architecture)

courses and/or conferences;
counselling;
reading of books and articles.

continued on page 126

time frame	Prolonged.	Short, intense.
staff requirements	Diagnostician; catalyst/facilitator; consultant helper; knowledge and skill in the dynamics of planned change; experience in the laboratory method of learning.	Teacher/trainer; programme manager; designer of training programmes; knowledge in the processes of human learning.
values	Humane and non-exploitative treatment of people or organisations; Theory Y assumptions; collaboration; sharing of power; rationality of behaviour; openness/candour/honesty; importance of surfacing and utilising conflict; right of persons and organisations to seek a full realisation of their potential; explicitness of values as a value in itself.	Competition; belief that 'education is progress'; belief that managers need challenging periodically; manager's right to have time for reflection and renewal; belief that individual should 'fit' organisation's needs; right of person to seek full realisation of his potential.

Adapted from Burke

Figure 21

A comparison of organisation development and management development

THE ROLE OF CAM

The Communicaton Advertising and Marketing Education Foundation Limited special courses on public relations and marketing communication have had an increasingly high uptake from all sections of industry and the service sector, despite the economic recession. There is evidence to suggest that management is increasingly appreciating the importance of specialised PR training, and this is reflected in the activities of organisations such as the Public Relations Consultants' Association, the Institution of Public Relations and, of course, the CAM Foundation itself.

CAM actually runs courses in two parts. The Certificate in Communication Studies, which is common to all subsequent Diploma specialisation, is the learning part of the education system and is aimed at providing what CAM calls accelerated experience. The Diploma stage is regarded as the opportunity to apply the knowledge gained at Certificate level to the solution of real life business problems. The full new syllabus is reproduced as Appendix 5 by permission of CAM. People in the public relations industry are happy to have a CAM course qualification. There is no doubt, looking through the guide of the Public Relations Consultants' Association, that even heads of public relations organisations are identifying themselves more and more readily as having a DipCAM or a Certificate from a CAM course. This is clearly seen to be an important development in the right direction.

It is always possible, however, to criticise. The CAM Foundation offers formal, official training in PR. It also trains marketing and advertising people. There is a great debate going on within the PR industry as to whether this form of training is the right one, because it is felt by some that the disciplines of marketing and advertising are not necessarily relevant to the adequate training of PR people. One of the most effective people on the PR training scene is Frank Jefkins, who has written many books and has proved the value of his practical, down-to-earth method of teaching people press relations, how to write a press release, how to meet deadlines, what you do in organising a press conference, how to organise print work, how to run special events, how to mobilise and organise an exhibition stand; all these practical matters are the nitty gritty work of the PR person at junior to middle level. That sort of training is quite different from the training of somebody who is concerned with analysing marketing opportunities.

Marketing people, as well as PR people, should understand the broad context in which the PR function operates, and this is where CAM performs a very important role. The danger is that the course teachers may not be really sure themselves how PR fits in; that can lead to people emerging with a CAM Diploma but not really knowing very much about the PR function. Many such students are frustrated because they do not really feel they have got to grips with the practical problems of PR, even if they are beginning to understand something about the marketing mix.

On the whole the CAM course in PR is making a valiant attempt at encouraging a multidisciplinary approach for those interested in the public relations function. The reason why some PR practitioners are not terribly impressed with the CAM courses in many cases is that they do not seem practical enough in their training. Although an effort has been made to bring in visiting lecturers with practical experience, all too often those who are teaching have very little practical experience of running public relations departments. The problem is that most practitioners are too busy and are not passing on their knowledge to the next generation. Teachers may be people who have not been terribly successful in the practical role.

The missing thing, perhaps, in terms of the public relations programme, is what is covered in more detail under communications practice. The creative aspects, the creative function, involve, according to CAM: the creative interpretation of what is to be communicated to whom, by what media and how; the liaison between the media and the creative production functions; how different media communicate with their audiences; the creative characteristics of the press, television, cinema and other media; how the medium affects the message; and choosing the right kind of message for each medium, and the production techniques that can help communicate it. They also look at the creative task as far as advertising is concerned, not really very much as far as the public relations area is concerned. This may be one of the most important areas for future development.

Creative interpretation is a very difficult subject to teach, but it could be more important than any other area and should at least have a separate paper in the public relations Diploma course. It needs to cover techniques for evaluating and appraising, and how to interpret current political, economical and social trends as they affect some of the specific audiences.

COURSES RUN BY OTHER ORGANISATIONS

If we accept, first, that public relations is increasingly being recognised as a specialist activity, and is becoming more visible and sophisticated and, secondly, that there is a growing need for some kind of formal thinking in public relations, what are the best vehicles for organising training?

As we have said, CAM plays a central role. There are now a large number of North American universities offering under-graduate courses in communications, which cover the theory and practice of public relations, marketing and advertising. Cranfield now offer a postgraduate course and other major UK universities may well follow suit; they may well begin by including practical PR as part of the communications studies aspect of degrees in business studies. Now, the ideal education and training is still held to embrace a degree in the arts or social sciences; a PPE or economics or sociology degree is regarded as an indicator of knowledge and analytical skills helpful in interpreting a rapidly changing political and socio-economic scene. A more vocationally guided course could well have appeal.

Meanwhile, more public relations consultancies are running their own training programmes. The CBI initiated training programmes for industry, particularly in the press relations area, which have been highly successful and very important. Other organisations are now running courses in communications, including the British Institute of Management. Large organisations like Barclays Bank and the larger financial institutions appreciate the importance of public relations and are allocating management time for the training function.

INCREASING PROFESSIONALISM

There is a rapidly growing awareness that public relations is no longer an amateur game. It is becoming increasingly specialist and sophisticated.

> Too many people tend to think that anybody can go and take a few journalists out to lunch, smile sweetly and pleasantly and entertain them and you get what you want. But it is not like that any more. There is much more research one needs to go into before you can actually project. Certainly this is so within the Civil Service.

Graduate recruitment has risen sharply, and public relations is now seen as a career prospect with professional respectability.

> Obviously there are characteristics which are common across all types of PR. But 'PR' really is such a generalisation. Product PR, for example, is so different from financial PR, or government PR, so you cannot really talk across the whole range.

> I have to admit there was a time when I would never admit to anybody that I was in PR. People used to get hostile, start dismissing one, which is so false, because of the sort of con-man image of PR.

But career progression is a problem in the PR industry. Most consultancies are small; in terms of organisation structure, they tend to be flat pyramids, with few layers, and hence limited opportunities for upward career progression through the hierarchy. Equally, there are few rungs up the promotion ladder in most in-house PR departments, the status of which very much depends on the view of PR taken by the organisation overall.

> That is very true within the Civil Service. Starting at the semi-clerical grade, going right up to the Chief Information Officer level, there are about six grades. There is always the argument in government that the person who is Information Officer is doing exactly the same as a Principal, and in fact possibly more. More of the work. Yet the grading system is rather cosmetic.

The criticism that too few well educated and well trained people are moving into public relations is still frequently made, but there is evidence of increasing professionalism and growing interest from people with professional career aspirations. The obvious remedy of offering rewarding career paths has now been widely recognised by the larger, publically quoted, PR companies. However, there is still not enough planning for careers in the public relations industry as a whole.

> What tends to happen in the PR business is that people come to it late. Either that or you start off young; there is no sort of happy medium. People come to it late having been in some sort of semi-journalistic career, and think that PR might be rather nice. And they'll dabble, and they come in late. Or you get the raw person, who comes in lower down but does not have much of a ladder to move up. The only ladder seems to be starting your own company, as it were.

But there are signs that solutions are being worked out.

> I have had one university graduate here with an arts degree for the last year, and I have made a specific attempt to train him into the needs of this job. And a year has gone by and he has just done it! It has worked out rather well. But I must say it is very exhausting to do the job and to do the training. So I do not think I would want to spend another year training in the same detailed way as I have done this time. But hopefully *he* can do it next time. I will then evaluate his success on his ability to train.

Job rotation is another exciting possibility.

> I have suggested, when the need has been apparent that we have someone else on the staff, that a line executive comes out of his job for a year, eighteen months or two years, spends the time here and then goes back. At the moment that has not been agreed to, but I think it will be in the future. It is normal in the States; they are much more flexible in their training.

HOW FEASIBLE IS FORMAL TRAINING?

Underlying all discussion on training in public relations is of course the fundamental question: to what extent can the necessary skills and abilities be acquired through any kind of formal programme?

> I do not think you can really. You could be taught how to write properly and how to take a scrappy brief and build it up, and present it as a press release. Or enlarge it or expand it. By doing exercises. But you cannot really be taught more than the basic mechanics of *how* to do it.

In this respect, the stuff of public relations falls reasonably easily into two parts. First, there is a basic orientation towards other people; empathetic qualities are essential to the job. 'If you do not have that basic sort of orientation, you might as well not bother.' Secondly, there is the craft aspect of the job; one draws a distinction between craft and art. And there clearly are aspects of the PR craft which can be taught. It is possible to teach that, through proper structuring and organising of the PR team, while one cannot eliminate 'half-past-five crises', the chances of their erupting can certainly be minimised. If, say, 90 per cent of activity is controlled, the system can probably accommodate 10 per cent of eruptions.

> I hope there is a degree of training but there will be experiences, a broad range of experiences, that with the training will make a PR man.

> As soon as you start training someone you are specialising . . . and losing the input that comes from those experiences. So that a nice combination of both would be nice. But on-the-job training and education really is the best possible thing for PR, I think.

Obviously, educational philosophies in a general sense will determine the nature and direction of training in public relations and broader attempts at management development. It seems plausible to suggest that real commitment to the role of PR is reflected in the level of resources allocated to the personal development of its staff.

> All of my section heads go to management training, to recognised management training courses. I am the only one that does not, because I reckon I have had mine outside and I really do not have the time. They all undergo this, and middle management, that is the senior information officers I have been talking about, they all undergo training too. The idea then is to gear them up to a point where they retain their professionalism, their specialism, but also manage their teams effectively.

> I am a great believer in giving people their chance. An example: a clerk who became a successful film director, first within the industry but now with outside recognition. That is satisfying to me. In terms of formal training, we have a residential Staff College – the high fliers go for six weeks of general management, broadening their knowledge of the industry, etc. We have a management development system in the Board, which is quite elaborate, and is taken quite seriously. Also, I have arranged for

132

people to swap jobs, either between the branches and Head Office or with other departments, the Department of Energy for instance. But only for a fortnight at a time; we agreed that was long enough. Evaluation of results? It is very useful for people working in London to see firsthand how branches operate.

But in PR training and management development, as in the practice of PR itself, there is still the inevitable search to produce, even if only implicitly, proof of cost effectiveness.

It pays off, because we know who is good and who is bad, because we have got reports on them. More importantly, we feel there are some guys who have come up very very well. Oh, extremely well, extremely well.

Well, it was useful. I did the old IPR exam many years ago, and it was good for me because it introduced me to whole areas which I was not working in at the time. I felt I was better as a result of it. I think, thinking about what you are doing and reading about what you are doing is never wasted anyway. I think that the problem comes, perhaps, in other terms. How valuable is it, for example, for an engineer to go and do another further degree instead of spending two years actually working in the firm? It is a more difficult thing than PR where the number of courses available is fairly small and you do not take off too much time.

Appendix 1

Checklist of problem areas

Identified Problem Area	Action			
	Currently under discussion	*Decision taken*	*Decision implemented*	*No action as yet*	*Shelved*

1. *Corporate planning*

1.1. Has the strategic decision yet been taken of whether either to stand still or to opt for continued development?

1.2. What decisions have been discussed/taken re: the investment of some £00,000 profits? To what extent have the full possibilities been researched (eg acquisitions? consultancy? property? bonds?)

1.3 What is company policy on new business, ie are other directors being actively encouraged to pursue/develop new business opportunities?

1.4. How are estimates reached of 'best' and 'worst' when planning for the organisation's future?

1.5. What rationale lay beneath the decision to seek a second account within the industry? How much research has been done into the industry's current performance and future prospects?

1.6. Obvious problem area to have come out of recent appraisal/review document: why has there been a higher turnover but the same level of profit? The problems need to be well understood and communicated to all members of the organisation.

2. *Organisational development*

2.1. What decisions have been reached about the future development of the organisational structure of the company?

2.2. Specifically, what steps have been taken to ensure that it can most effectively receive prospective new business accounts?
How much thought has been expended on the process of getting new business, from the initial stage of searching for new business opportunities to the point where new business is incorporated into the organisational structure?

Identified Problem Area	Action				
	Currently under discussion	Decision taken	Decision implemented	No action as yet	Shelved
2.3. How much improvement has there been over the past six-month period in lateral communications?					
2.4. What are the reasons for this?					
(a) less centralised control by the Chairman and Managing Director?					
(b) increased appreciation of the need for lateral communications?					
(c) conscious effort to make the necessary time despite high work pressure?					
2.5. What are the implications of this?					
2.6. Has a situation arisen where an ad hoc project coordinator has been appointed?					
2.7. What mechanisms/processes have been developed to foresee and to manage changes in the environment?					
2.8. Could it be said that the company has now moved successfully from the pioneering to the integrative stage of organisational development?					

2.9. Is there now a greater 'sense of organisation' within the company?

2.10. What has been done to reduce the incidence of role conflict and ambiguity, and to make the effect of these conditions (when they cannot be avoided) minimally damaging to the person and to the organisation? Which of these possibilities have been used?

(a) introduction of direct structural change;

(b) introduction of new criteria of selection and placement;

(c) increasing the tolerance and coping qualities of individuals;

(d) strengthening the interpersonal bonds among members of the organisation.

3. *Role of the Board and Management Group*

3.1. Have the roles and terms of reference of the Board and the Management Group now been clearly defined, by some participative process?

Identified Problem Area	Action				
	Currently under discussion	Decision taken	Decision implemented	No action as yet	Shelved
3.2. Have the following crucial relationships been clearly defined, by some participative process?					
(a) the relationship between the Board and the Management Group?					
(b) the relationship between the Board and the Chairman and Managing Director/principal shareholder?					
(c) the relationship between the Management Group and the other members of the organisation?					
3.3. Has there been any reduction in the ambiguity previously surrounding the role of Board Director?					
4. *Role of the Chairman and Managing Director*					
4.1. Have the two functions of *maintenance* (routine administrative work) and *adaptation* (the generation of new business and the					

formulation of strategic plans) been, so far as is practicable, separated? Is the Chairman able to devote most of his energy to the second function, adaptation?

4.2. Has the *behaviour* of the Chairman and Managing Director changed to the extent that it now better fits the new *structure* of his role?

4.3. Has the Chairman yet decided whether he is to become Chairman or Chief Executive of the company?

5. *Role of the Chairman's deputy/No. 2 man*

5.1 What decisions have been discussed/ implemented about the role of the Chairman's deputy/No. 2 man vis à vis

(a) the Chairman and Managing Director;

(b) the Directors of other groups;

(c) executives within Division A.

5.2. What efforts has he made toward the ordering of priorities vis à vis competing demands upon his time?

Identified Problem Area	Currently under discussion	Decision taken	Action Decision implemented	No action as yet	Shelved
5.3. How has his allocation of time/priorities among the several aspects of his role changed over the past few months?					
6. *Role of Y*					
What decisions have been discussed/ implemented about the Role of Y?					
6.1. To what extent is it intended to develop Y?					
6.2. Is it considered that he will be promoted into his boss's current role, as and when he becomes Assistant Managing Director, ie effectively the No. 2?					
7. *Recruitment of a new executive into Division A*					
7.1. By what processes have the new executive's role, role set and terms of reference been defined?					
7.2. What will be the relationship between the new executive and the Chairman? Will he					

have a direct reporting link to the No. 2, and to the No. 2 only?

7.3. On which accounts will he be working?

7.4. What steps will be taken to ensure that the currently existing '2-camp situation' is not perpetuated through this new recruit?
The recruiting of a suitably qualified woman for this role could do much to reduce the tension. Currently all divisions run parallel, ie the male/female divide reflects exactly the Consumer Group/Industrial Group divide.)

7.5. The Chairman has said in discussion that the big advantage of bringing in this new person is that 'he will be purpose-built for the job, so we can avoid any problems right from the start.' What problems could be expected to arise?

(a) Ambiguity re: roles of account directors, account executives. This should be clarified from the beginning. How will this be done?

(b) Chairman's involvement: would it be preferable for the Chairman not to get

Identified Problem Area	Action				
	Currently under discussion	Decision taken	Decision implemented	No action as yet	Shelved
involved with the new executive's work, but to rely completely on feedback reports from his No. 2?					
7.6. The Chairman has said in discussion that he will bear the initial costs of this new executive, 'so that a wise decision may be made from the organisation's point of view'. Surely this will then be shown as an overhead, which will have to be borne in part by all groups within the company? If so, how has this been presented to the other directors?					
8. *Role of staff personnel*					
8.1. What action has been taken to reduce the ambiguity in the roles of staff personnel?					
9. *Internal processes*					
9.1. In what ways have the internal control					

systems been improved during the last six-month period?

9.2. Has there been any change in the level of morale within the company over the last six-month period?

Have there been any visible indications that morale is either improving or weakening?

What positive steps have been initiated in order to attempt to improve motivation?

9.3. What efforts have been made to increase the levels of openness and trust within the company? Has any progress been made?

9.4. What efforts have been made to improve the level of feedback to individuals about their work?

Appendix 2

Checklist for evaluating and reviewing on-going relationships with clients

Potential problem area	Evaluation of current situation			Actual performance measured against budgeted forecasts		Action			
	Good	Satisfactory	Unsatisfactory	Actual	Budgeted	Currently under discussion	Decision taken	Decision implemented	No action as yet
1. *Time input*									
1.1. Client liaison									
• meetings									
• telephone									
• written									
1.2. Press liaison									
• preparing releases									
• selling releases									
• distributing releases									
• press conferences									

1.3. Special events (specify)

1.4. Planning

1.5. Reporting

1.6. Miscellaneous

2. *Costs*

2.1. Fixed costs

2.2. Variable costs

3. *Role definition*

3.1. Is there any ambiguity in the definition of the specialist's role?

3.2. Is there any conflict in the definition of the specialist's role?

3.3. Is there clear communication of role expectations between specialists and the client?

145

Potential problem area	Evaluation of current situation			Actual performance measured against budgeted forecasts		Action			
	Good	Satisfactory	Unsatisfactory	Actual	Budgeted	Currently under discussion	Decision taken	Decision implemented	No action as yet
3.4. Has the specialist's role developed in any way since the beginning of the relationship?									
4. Campaign effectiveness									
4.1. Have campaigns mounted for the client been successful? Why?									
4.2. What results have the campaign(s) achieved?									

5. *Evaluation of creative input*

5.1. What level of innovation has gone into the campaign(s)?

5.2. To what extent has the campaign(s) been characterised by 'new' activities/ideas?

6. *Implementation*

6.1. Has the campaign(s) been well organised? What criticisms could be made?

6.2. Have resources been used in an optimal way?

6.3. Was the planning of the campaign satisfactory? Eg have any problems/panics/ omissions arisen which

Potential problem area	Evaluation of current situation			Actual performance measured against budgeted forecasts		Action			
	Good	Satisfactory	Unsatisfactory	Actual	Budgeted	Currently under discussion	Decision taken	Decision implemented	No action as yet
could have perhaps been avoided with more careful planning?									
6.4. Has there been good cooperation with the client?									
6.5. Has there been good cooperation with the press?									
6.6. Has the campaign been well integrated									
(a) so as to provide a coherent 'plan of attack'?									
(b) within the specialist department/ consultancy?									

148

(c) with the activities
of the client
organisation?

(d) with the press?

(e) with other
external
organisations, eg
advertising
agencies?

7. *Is the approach proactive?*

Has the approach been
proactive rather than
reactive?

Does the specialist
department/consultancy
take the initiative vis à vis
making contact with:

(a) the client?

(b) the press?

(c) other external
organisations, eg the
public etc?

149

Potential problem area	Evaluation of current situation			Actual performance measured against budgeted forecasts		Action			
	Good	Satisfactory	Unsatisfactory	Actual	Budgeted	Currently under discussion	Decision taken	Decision implemented	No action as yet
8. Communication									
8.1. Is the message being communicated?									
8.2. Is the message being communicated to the right people?									
8.3. Is the message being received? How can this be proven?									
8.4. What is happening as a result of that message being communicated and received?									

9. *Optimal use of resources*

   Are resources being used effectively according to the following formula: given the *process* of the PR activity, is the *output* satisfactory vis à vis the *input*? Eg are the right staff being used for the right jobs?

10. *Summary*

   Has the campaign to date been effective from the point of view of the specialist?

10.1. Have there so far been any indications of latent dissatisfaction from the client?

10.2. What are the prospects for renewal of the account?

10.3. Is the account currently profitable?

Appendix 3

Subjective questionnaire for use in evaluating and reviewing ongoing relationships with clients

These questions are intentionally open-ended and non-directive, so as to elicit as far as possible the client's precise feelings.

Examples should be encouraged wherever possible, for example: 'Well, I thought the consultancy should really have done X, Y and Z without our having to ask them.'

1. In which areas are you most satisfied with your present relationship with the consultancy?
2. In which areas are you least satisfied with your present relationship with the consultancy?
3. Are there any of the consultancy's activities which you would like it to do differently?
4. Would you like the consultancy to do anything else which it does not do now?
5. Would you prefer the consultancy *not* to do something which it does now?
6. How would you try to alter the consultancy's behaviour to fit your own expectations/preferences better?
7. Do you think that the consultancy is clear about your own level of satisfaction with the present campaign(s)?
8. Does the consultancy usually make itself clear when it wants or expects something from you?

9. Do you think the consultancy is clear about your own expectations of their involvement in your organisation?

Appendix 4

Specimen activity record

Name ....

Date ....

Activity number	Client	Type of activity							Other people involved			Initiation		Channel			Regularity			Time (minutes)		
		Client liaison	Press release	Press conference	Special event	Planning	Reporting	Miscellaneous	Own staff	Client	External	Initiated by self	Initiated by client	Meeting	Telephone	Written	Regular	Ad hoc	Interruption	0–5	5–30	30+
1																						
2																						
3																						
4																						

Appendix 4

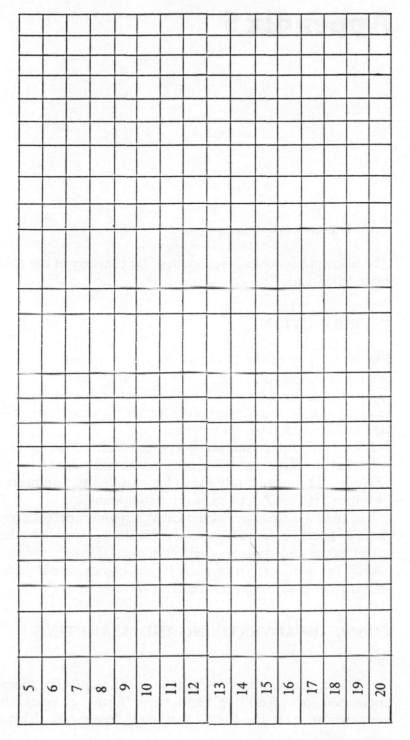

Appendix 5

CAM Diploma syllabus

The following syllabus is reproduced by courtesy of the CAM Foundation Ltd.

INTRODUCTION

The philosophy of the Diploma stage is that students should acquire the expertise to apply the knowledge gained at Certificate level to the solution of real business problems. Both the teaching and the examinations are largely by 'case study', thus simulating actual business practice.

A wide range of ten subjects is available from which a student will select any three, this being the minimum required for a pass Diploma. The opportunity exists for a further two subjects to be taken, thus leading to an Honours Diploma.

The modular structure of the CAM Diploma enables candidates to select those areas of study directly applicable to their career needs and those of their employer. Those wishing to qualify for membership of professional bodies should obtain information as to entry requirements directly from them.

CONSUMER ADVERTISING AND MARKETING

Aim

Candidates are expected to show a grasp of the general application of advertising (and other forms of marketing communication) to the overall marketing framework. This is, above all, a communication examination with the emphasis on communication within the marketing mix, rather than on marketing in total. Candidates must demonstrate a knowledge of the marketing environment into which communications will fit: they will also be expected to show that they are current in terms of practice.

Objectives

- To provide students with an understanding of the elements of marketing communication planning
- To examine the elements of the Marketing Communication plan, the media and research for and evaluation of the plan
- To show the organisation for advertising
- To illustrate the above with concrete samples.

General

- The role of publicity and communication within an overall marketing prgramme
- The establishment of precise advertising, publicity and promotion objectives
- The development of advertising strategies.

Campaign Planning

- The evaluation of communication problems and the co-ordinated use of all available advertising methods, both media and creative, for problem solving. In particular, the steps needed to construct a total communication programme.

Budgeting

- The establishment of budgets for consumer communication programmes.

The Promotional Mix

- The inter-relation of above-the-line and below-the-line techniques

- How promotion may be built into marketing and communication strategies.

Research and Evaluation

- The use of research within a communication programme. Tracking Studies
- How to evaluate the elements of an advertising and promotional plan.

Organisation

- Organisation for advertising
- Agency/client relationship
- Types of advertising structure wtihin companies.

Reading List

Essential
Complete Guide to Advertising
Douglas; Macmillan
Advertising: what it is and how to do it
White; McGraw Hill

Supplementary
Advertising Works (Vols I & II)
Broadbent; Hall-Saunders
Advertising Works (Vol. III)
Channon; Hall-Saunders
20 Advertising Case Histories
IPA; Holt Rinehart & Winston

Other
Marketing Management
Kotler; Prentice Hall
Advertising Law
Lawson; M & E, Pitman

INDUSTRIAL ADVERTISING AND MARKETING

Aim

To show the practice of industrial marketing and advertising, with emphasis on the planning of integrated campaigns. The way the industrial marketing operation is organised in companies, and the methods of obtaining facts about the market place. The different types of communication channels and the data available to assess them. The place of public relations in industrial marketing, and the relations with other industrial communications.

Objectives

- To show the role of communication in the context of the Industrial Marketing Communication campaign
- To examine the steps involved in designing an Industrial Marketing Communication campaign
- To describe and examine the role of Research, Media and Public Relations as part of the Industrial Communication campaign
- To describe the role of supplier organisations.

General

- The role of communication in the context of the industrial marketing plan
- The differences between industrial (or business-to-business) and consumer purchasing, and the variations in purchasing patterns, the decision making unit and buying influences within industry for different types of product
- The importance of setting clear precise communication objectives from which integrated, multi-media campaigns are planned for product, service or corporate advertising
- How much should be spent: methods of determining budgets based on up to date knowledge of costs and appreciation of the size of budgets normally required to promote industrial goods
- Measuring the results and cost-effectiveness of different types of communication activity
- Legal and voluntary restraints which must be considered when planning an industrial campaign.

Company Organisation

- Types of marketing and publicity structures within industrial companies: identifying buying influences and their relative importance for different types of products and methods of distribution. The role of the sales force and the contribution made by distributors or sales agents in communication.

Research

- Industrial marketing research: sources of information and techniques for desk research
- Application of the Standard Industrial Classification (SIC) system
- Evaluation of sales and measuring advertising effectiveness.

Media

- The strengths and weaknesses of *all* types of media for industrial advertising – press (newspapers, weekly periodicals, magazines, trade and technical and professional journals); literature; direct mail; exhibitions; films; television; radio; outdoor advertising; telephone selling; point of sale and audio-visual material
- A broad knowledge of current levels of costing in each of these areas.

Media Research

- Qualitative and quantitative methods of assessing readership and circulation
- The Industrial Media Data Form (MDF) and the Exhibition Data Form (EDF) – both administered by the Audit Bureau of Circulation (ABC)
- The limitations of standard research reports as a guide to media selection
- Data specifically prepared for industrial use.

Public Relations

- The place of public and press relations in industrial communications
- Organisation of press conferences, demonstrations and facility visits
- Internal and external house journals.

Supplier Organisations

- Advertising agencies – contracts and agreements
- Exhibition organisers and contractors
- Direct mail agents
- Sales promotion consultancies
- Printers.

Reading List

Essential
Business-to-Business Advertising
Norman Hart; Associated Business Press
The Fundamentals of Advertising
John Wilmshurst; Heinemann

Supplementary
Guide to Industrial Publicity
(ISBA)
Marketing Digest
Fred Polhill; (quarterly) magazine
Business Marketing
(monthly); Crain Communications, USA

Other
Guide for Exhibitors
(ISBA)
Guide to Direct Mail Advertising
(ISBA)
How to Succeed in Advertising (1–5)
(IPA)
How to Organize Effective Conferences and Meetings
David Seekings; Kogan Page
The Marketing of Industrial Products
Norman Hart; McGraw Hill

INTERNATIONAL ADVERTISING AND MARKETING

Introduction

The course is designed to examine variations in marketing and advertising practice when applied in more than one country.

Primary emphasis is placed on advertising and marketing in the countries of your own region so that the lessons learned can be developed in some depth. But the underlying objective of the course is to extend principles to global marketing considerations.

Aims

The aim is for students to learn how to succeed in marketing and advertising products and services internationally covering the organisation and all sales facets. Part of the course is necessarily devoted to gaining knowledge, but students should also understand its practical applications and will be examined on this in the form of a case study.

Objectives

On completion students should know how to approach international markets and how to decide which or what market. They should know how first to enter a market and how to react within an established market from both an organisational and marketing standpoint, understanding the country-by-country and the pan-country international approach. Global organisation and marketing now affect all walks of life and students should be aware of their importance and their implications.

The objective is for students not simply to know the marketing possibilities, but also to be able to assess and create a plan for marketing internationally with realistic goals and budgets which can be justified.

International Marketing Background

Strategy and Organisation for Marketing Abroad
- How to develop into an overseas market
- Principal factors determining market organisation, product market, company structure

162

- Types of structure – sales agent, export sales department, offices abroad, advantages/disadvantages of global organisation
- International Marketing Planning – market differences, product, pricing, sales support, cost, profit
- Methods of handling promotion overseas.

Market Characteristics

- Basic economic advertising facts about countries in your region; industry, language, media available, limitations on products and sales activities, competition.

Intelligence for Marketing Abroad

- Categories of information required/available
- Sources and uses of information
- Practical limitations
- Sources of desk research
- Special applications for international marketing
- Special techniques
- Size of markets and their demographics.

International Communication Practice

- Communication strategy and co-ordination
- Appropriate degrees of co-ordination
- Advantages
- The co-ordinator's role in, and outside, the marketing company.

Research for International Advertising

- Special problems overseas, comparison, pan-frontier
- Sources
- Techniques.

Advertising Agency Organisation

- Types of agency structure
- Relationship with client structure
- Problems of exclusivity
- Remuneration
- Agency/client contracts.

Advertising Media

- Characteristics of individual media
- International media
- Media buying practice
- Media data.

Media Research

- Availability/usage.

Creating the Plan

- Budgeting
- Control
- Assessment
- Extending the plan forward to enable assessment of expenditure, potential market share, success, profit, market and organisational development.

Advertising Creative

- Methods of producing overseas advertising
- Quality control
- Translation
- Local regulations affecting advertising.

Reading List

Essential
Case studies in International Marketing
P Doyle and N A Hart; Heinemann
International Marketing
Stanley J Paliwoda; Heinemann

Supplementary
International Marketing
L S Walsh; M&E Handbooks
Focus
(monthly); Crain Communications
Media International
(monthly).

PR FOR COMMERCIAL ORGANISATIONS

Introduction

The syllabus is designed on the assumption that students have learned the basic skills and how to apply them to reach various publics through the appropriate media.

This paper demands the exercise of judgement, an awareness of the opportunities (and limitations) for public relations within the context of a business, and the use of public relations techniques to contribute both to achieving specific tasks and to the broader aspects of sound commercial practice.

Aim

This paper is intended to test the ability of the public relations practitioner, to demonstrate how positive corporate perception may be established, to maintain and to assess the candidate's suitability for executive status in a business world that depends increasingly upon effective, clear communication.

Objectives

- To describe and examine the process and PR activity for creating corporate awareness campaigns and developing employee communication activities
- To describe the process of PR activity in relation to financial Public Relations, Government relations and local communities
- To show the role of PR in support of marketing activity.

Corporate Awareness

- Definition of corporate identity, culture, positioning and reputation; influencing factors
- Identification of publics and measurement of opinions, attitudes and motives
- Formulating a corporate awareness programme
- The projection of a corporate awareness
- The integration of all aspects of PR activity to achieve this end and to:

— enhance long term awareness among its key publics of a company's aims and achievements
— foster favourable attitudes and minimise unfavourable actions due to lack of information.

Employee Communications

The role of the PR practitioner in developing in-house awareness and appreciation of the company's policies, products and services. Information gathering and dissemination, relationships with personnel, training, industrial relations, marketing and line management, in emergency procedures and in internal communications.

Financial Public Relations

- The role of PR in the raising of capital (for companies). Maintaining the confidence of a company's shareholders, investment analysts, commentators by a regular flow of information on aims and achievements
- Dealing with special situations such as take-overs and mergers, transferring from private to public company, privatisation, Management buy outs
- Stock exchange procedures and regulations
- International capital markets – PR strategies related to international quotations and fund raising.

Government Relations

- Understanding the legislative processes in Westminster and Whitehall, the role of parliament including government and opposition parties and the system by which laws are made; appreciating the responsibilities of the EEC Commission, the European Parliament and the administrative bodies; responsibility for the development of EEC directives and transnational law
- Establishing and maintaining relationships with relevant individuals and officials within these organisations
- Monitoring the development of legislation and undertaking the presentation of the case relevant to proposed parliamentary actions that affect the business activity

- The role of trade associations, professional bodies, business organisations and pressure groups in parliamentary relations.

Local Communities

- The importance of the local populace, and especially key sub-groups, being kept aware of the company's attitudes and policies
- Local communities as employees, customers, neighbours – past and present
- Involvement in local activities, on a personal and corporate level, as an aspect of corporate PR
- The need for regular planned communication with local government (elected members and permanent staff), local organisations and groups, local opinion formers (including local press, TV and radio)
- the inter-relationship between community and government relations programmes.

Public Relations in Support of Marketing

- The inter-relationships between PR and other functions in the marketing mix
- Ethical considerations, consumerism, consumer protection legislation
- Reaching mass consumer markets, contrasted and compared with market segments and specialised markets (eg for industrial products)
- The role of PR in communicating 'fair dealing' policies
- The role of PR in export marketing; the special PR problems of exporting and importing.

Reading List

Candidates sitting the PR Diploma papers are advised to read as widely as possible. The following books are of value in developing an in-depth knowledge of the subjects:
Company Image and Reality
David Bernstein; Holt, Rinehart & Winston
Doing Business in the European Community
John Drew; Butterworth

Local Government for Journalists
Geoffrey Smith; LGC Communications
McNae's Essential Law for Journalists
(eds) Walter Greenwood and Tom Welsh; Butterworth
Managing Corporate Relations
George S Moore; Gower Press
The Media in Britain
Jeremy Tunstall; Constable
Planned Press and Public Relations
Frank Jefkins; Blackie
Public Relations is Your Business
Colin Coulson-Thomas; Business Books
Successful Media Relations: A Practitioner's Guide
Judith Ridgway; Gower
The Practice of Public Relations
Wilfred Howard; Heinemann
All About PR
Roger Haywood; McGraw Hill
Public Relations – A Practical Guide
Colin Coulson-Thomas; M & E Handbook
This PR Consultancy Business
N. Mendes; Mendes 1984
Financial Marketing and Communications
Kain Newman; Holt, Rinehart and Winston.

PR FOR NON-COMMERCIAL ORGANISATIONS

Introduction

Non-commercial organisations are those whose principle purpose is not commercial. They are not organisations without financial and management disciplines nor are they necessarily non-profit making. This paper demands a clear appreciation of the PR opportunities and limitations of such organisations including:

- Membership organisations – professional bodies, trade associations, clubs, Housing Associations and Friendly Societies

- Government and government agencies – national, local and international
- Campaigning organisations – pressure and minority interest groups
- Quangos: quasi-autonomous non-government organisations
- Community, youth and special interest groups and voluntary organisations
- Religious groups and organisations
- Charities, including criteria and constraints of charitable status
- Political parties; trade unions
- Education bodies, authorities; Trusts
- Public utilities
- Broadcasting authorities – BBC, IBA.

Aim

The syllabus is designed to provide an awareness and understanding of the use of public relations in and for non-commercial organisations. It assumes that students already have thorough knowledge of the basic skills and techniques of public relations.

Objectives

- To describe the PR opportunities and limitations for a variety of non-commercial organisations
- To show the PR practice for each of these organisational types
- To examine the role of a number of organisations relative to non-commercial organisations, eg Charity Commission.

PR Practice for each organisation type:

- Identification of publics; measurement of opinions, attitudes and motives
- Formulating PR programmes for non-commercial organisations; setting PR objectives; programme elements; evaluation and reporting

- Employee communications – including voluntary staff and membership communications
- Budget criteria and controls; sources of funds; fund raising
- Government relations – influencing legislation; lobbying
- Community relations
- International relations
- Media relations.

An awareness of the roles of the Charity Commission, the Parliamentary Commissioner (ombudsman), the local government and health service ombudsmen, the National Council for Voluntary Organisations, the National Consumer Council and consumer consultative groups for the public utilities will be required; the organisation and structure of national and local government must be understood thoroughly.

Reading List

See *PR for Commercial Organisations*.

PR STRATEGY

Introduction

This paper is about the managerial role of the PR practitioner. It requires an understanding of how organisations set objectives, develop plans and integrate operations in pursuance of a defined strategy.

Public relations is driven by, and is supportive of, business or organisational strategy. It is concerned with the way an organisation behaves, and with the manner in which it explains itself to, and wins support from, stakeholder groups and other important publics in a multi-cultural society.

Aim

Successful implementation of PR strategy requires cohesive and co-ordinated effort by a senior management team, which relies on the PR practitioner's planning ability, judgement, and tactical awareness – especially in relation to short-term threats and opportunities. An understanding of the financial and organisational structure of an organisation, and cost and budgeting processes is essential. Passing of the paper will indicate that the candidate is capable of a senior executive level appointment in public relations.

Objectives

- To describe and examine the general practice of PR strategy
- To examine the role of the case study approach as a method to enhance knowledge and practical experience of PR
- To illustrate PR strategy practice with current examples.

General Practice

- The place of PR in the overall management function
- Identification of management disciplines and knowledge of how each contributes to the total enterprise
- The importance of long-term planning
- The continuous application of public relations techniques
- The analysis of circumstances or a special problem in order to identify how public relations techniques can best be applied
- The definition of public relations objectives in terms of changing or reinforcing public perceptions of an organisation
- The preparation and presentation of public relations budgets, proposals and programmes including evaluation methods
- The management and implementation of public relations programmes by means of a carefully scheduled and monitored series of activities
- Awareness of the development of public affairs practice in the establishment of relationships between business and the community
- Knowledge of the principles of corporate social responsibility
- Special considerations for the practice of PR on an international basis

- The particular PR strategy and management problems of multi-national companies
- The requirements for contingency planning and crisis management.

Case Study Practice

To enhance students' knowledge and practical experience of PR strategy, planning, costing, practice and evaluation.

Students should keep abreast of current news items and regularly read the financial and political pages of the press. Case studies are likely to be related to recent events.

Reading List

See *PR for Commercial Organisations*.

MANAGEMENT RESOURCES

Aim

The aim of this syllabus is to ensure that candidates have a broad understanding of modern management procedures (with particular reference to marketing, advertising and public relations practice in both commercial and non-commercial organisations) which will assist them in their own career development and in their day-to-day dealings with others.

Objectives

- To examine and describe the infrastructure of management and the duties of a manager
- To describe the elements and technique of effective personnel management and management accounting
- To examine the process of management planning
- To describe the role of computers in management.

Background to Management

- Definitions
- Company structure
- Management functions

172

- Management techniques
- Duties, responsibilities and inter-relationship of senior management.

Effective Personnel Management

- The human element
- Styles of personnel management
- The role of trade unions
- Formal and informal organisations
- Need for mutual understanding and co-operation
- Line and staff management
- Internal communication
- Recruitment and selection procedures
- Remuneration and incentives.

Management Accounting

- Sales forecasting
- Budgeting
- Standard costing: variances
- Responsibility accounting
- Allocation of overheads
- Pricing policies
- Costing and charging methods for service organisations (including non-commercial organisations).

Computers in Management

- What computers can and cannot do
- Use as a management tool
- Computers in action – it is intended that students will be given a limited amount of practical instruction.

Management Planning

- Problem identification
- Goal setting
- Corporate objectives
- Drawing up and presenting the plan
- Feed back
- Cybernetics.

Reading List

Essential
Practice of Management
Drucker; Heinemann
Insight into Management Accounting
Sizer; Penguin

Supplementary
Economics for Managers
Crowson and Richards; Macmillan

Other
Statistics in Action
Sprent; Penguin

MARKETING STRATEGY

Introduction

The purpose of this paper is to provide the vital strategic context within which lies the motivation and logic of communication activity. Good understanding of and familiarity with basic marketing concepts is taken for granted. How that understanding is applied in practical situations should be the student's major concern.

Aim

To examine the means by which a business or business unit of any kind can be defined and so indicate its scope, should determine its direction in the light of the environment in which it operates and its range of competences and resources, and can achieve the profit and other needs of stakeholders in the business in furthering its provision of benefits to the consumer.

Objectives

- To provide students with an understanding of the importance of the strategic audit and its value in developing strategies
- To examine the part played by the Marketing Director in representing the needs of the consumer throughout the organisation

174

- To indicate the value of integrated planning approaches in co-ordinating strategic business plans, marketing operational plans and functional plans for elements in the marketing mix with particular reference to communication planning
- To develop understanding of the central importance of differentiation, segmentation and positioning
- To examine the interaction between marketing and new product development
- To look at the special considerations surrounding international marketing
- To review marketing's place in the broad economy and various aspects of social, moral and ethical responsibility.

The Role of the Marketing Director in Corporate Development

- Effect of size upon organisation and tasks of management
- Delegation of Chief Executive responsibilities
- Responsibility v authority
- Place of marketing departments
- Organising the marketing department for effective input
- The co-ordinating role.

Setting Objectives

- Types of objective: comparative ratios, cash oriented, sales oriented, preserving status quo, 'comfortable' objectives
- Short v long-term objectives
- Target returns and recovery objectives.

Determining Strategy

- Defining market sectors
- Identifying opportunities
- Matching company skills to opportunities
- Strategies for different types of objectives
- When to change strategy
- Basic marketing stances
- Basic marketing strategy options
- Types of strategy

- Strategy for size, growth, change in corporate style
- Growth and diversification
- Growth by development, integration, acquisition.

Buying Behaviour

- Consumer behaviour
- Group behaviour
- Industrial buying
- Effect of buying behaviour on strategy and tactics
- Buying behaviour and advertising
- Buying behaviour and personal selling
- Buying behaviour and promotional effectiveness.

Identifying Opportunities

- Using market research to identify opportunities
- Research techniques
- Brand mapping
- Segmentation studies
- Gap analysis
- Life cycle opportunities
- Finding opportunities in hard times.

Differentiation and Segmentation

- Definitions
- Types of differentiation
- Differentiation and price
- Types of segmentation
- Segmentation and price
- Matching company stance to differentiation/ segmentation opportunities
- Identifying opportunity segments
- Finding growth segments in declining markets.

Marketing Mix Strategy

- The mix concept
- Components
- Key components for different businesses
- Specific areas:
    Channel strategy

Sales strategy
Advertising and promotional strategy
Product and product presentation strategy
Price strategies
Physical distribution strategies
- Changing strategy to reflect changing conditions, eg labour availability, rents, costs in general, changes in buying behaviour etc

New Product Development

- Role of the marketing department
- Fundamental v market-based research
- Strategies for effective new product development
- Role of research in new product development
- Role of PR in new product development
- Types of research available
- Co-ordination for effective new product development
- NPD related to growth objectives
- NPD related to life cycle stages
- NPD related to company strategy
- NPD v acquisition (buy or build).

Marketing Planning

- Components in the plan
- Sequences for effective planning
- Co-ordinating role for the marketing department
- Portfolio planning
- Role of forecasting in marketing planning
- Strategies into tactics
- Ensuring effective action after planning
- Keeping to the plan
- Changing plan v changing tactics to achieve the plan
- Effect of change on plans
- Short v long-term planning
- Long-range planning
- Impact of short-term change on long-term plans
- Impact of long-range plans on present actions
- Planning for profit
- Strategies for improving profits.

International Marketing

- Reasons for marketing internationally
- Growth through international marketing
- International marketing v exporting; Organisational strategies: multi-national, international, export
- Role of PR as precursor in foreign markets
- Head-office v local marketing
- Marketing departments and marketing services
- Profit strategies for multi-nationals
- Advertising strategies in international marketing
- Price strategies in international marketing
- Channel strategies in international marketing
- Product design and naming strategies
- Differences between local and international marketing
- Strategies that take account of differences.

Marketing and the Economy

- Marketing as the voice of the consumer
- Legal and social obligations of marketing departments/ use of PR to meet those obligations
- Accepting product liability
- Guarantees, after-sales service, spares etc
- Socially acceptable behaviour:
     product pollution
     prices
     profit levels
     effect on others (lead in petrol, for example)
- Role of marketing in economic growth
- Effect of economic restraint upon company growth
- Growth opportunities in economic developments.

Reading List

Essential
Marketing: Planning, Analysis and Control
Philip Kotler; Prentice Hall International Editions
Managing for Results
P F Drucker; Pan Management Series

Supplementary
Product Management
P Doyle et al; Harper and Row
Behavioural Aspects of Marketing
K C Williams; Heinemann/IM/CAM

Other
New Products and Diversification
P F Kraushar; Business Books
Also important are periodicals such as *Marketing*, *Marketing Week* and *Harvard Business Review* especially for up-to-date case histories and state-of-the-art techniques.

MARKET RESEARCH

Introduction

The course builds on the introduction to marketing research provided by the CAM Research and Behavioural Studies Certificate Course.

Aim

On completion of the Diploma course students should be fully aware of the role of research in communication, advertising and marketing, and have a detailed understanding of all facets of the research process, including its management and control.

Objectives

- To examine the structure of the marketing research industry
- To describe and examine the role of the professional standards, legal and self regulatory controls
- To describe the steps involved in marketing research methodology
- To examine specific applications of marketing research to the marketing mix
- To examine the management of the research function.

Structure of Marketing Research Industry

- The historical development of marketing research from its origins in the UK and USA to its worldwide extension
- The relative importance of marketing research in consumer goods and services, industrial goods and services, retailing, international trade, public opinion, government, social problems
- Structure of the marketing research industry and the role of: company, agency/consultancy, academic researchers.

Professional Standards, Legal and Self-Regulatory Controls

- The role of professional research bodies (eg MRS, IMRA, SRA, ESOMAR)
- Legal constraints (eg data privacy), self-regulatory controls (eg MRS Code of Conduct, identity card schemes).

The Research Approach to Marketing Problems

- Identifying consumer, industrial and social marketing problems and information needs
- The measurement of market sizes, structure and trends; identification of target customers, their needs and consumption patterns
- The research approach, designing research programmes.

Marketing Information Systems

- The role of secondary data and desk research. Coping with the 'information explosion'. Integrating in-company, syndicated research, market survey and external published data
- The approach to searching and evaluating published sources
- Main sources of secondary data including: Government, official, trade, media, academic, commercial, and syndicated (eg BARB, JICNARS, TGI)
- Information technology (on-line numeric and bibliographic databases, freeform and keyword search, videotex, microfiche).

Primary Field Research

- Qualitative research techniques, benefits and limitations
- Quantitative data collection methods (personal, telephone, mail)
- Attitude and brand image measurement
- Principles of questionnaire design
- Theory and practice of sampling
- Fieldwork, interviewing, field quality control
- Non-interactive research methods
- Panels, audits, omnibus surveys, test centres
- Electronic apparatus for data collection by interviewers and respondents.

Data Analysis and Presentation of Findings

- Techniques of data collation and analysis
- Data coding, editing and analysis specification for computers. Batch and interactive methods
- Statistical techniques in the analysis and interpretation of survey data
- Sampling error, bias and validation
- Forecasting and simulation models
- Report writing and personal presentation.

Application of Research to the Marketing Mix

- Product, name, package testing
- Advertising research: setting objectives, developing and pre-testing advertising approaches, media selection, measuring the effectiveness of campaigns
- Research in the preparation and evaluation of sales promotion and public relations programmes
- Research for pricing, distribution methods and selling
- Evaluation of new products and services, test marketing, monitoring a market launch
- Research for the media: editorial/programme content and audience.

Management of the Research Function

- Division of work and relationships between in-company research departments and outside agencies/consultancies

- Selecting and briefing the research agency
- The research proposal: its content and evaluation for cost-effectiveness
- Controlling a survey
- Organising multi-national studies
- Utilisation of research results and their application to marketing.

Reading List

Essential
Marketing Research Process
M Crimp; Prentice Hall, 2nd Edition, 1986
Survey Research Practice
G Hoinville and R Jowell; Heinemann, 1978
Code of Conduct
Market Research Society, 1986

Supplementary
Manual of Industrial Marketing Research
(ed) A Rawnsley; Wiley, 1978
Marketing Research for Managers
S Crouch; Heinemann, 1984

Other
Standardised Questions
(ed) A Wolfe; Market Research Society, 2nd edition, 1985
A Primer in Data Reduction
A Ehrenberg; Wiley, 1983
Testing to Destruction
A Hedges; Institute of Practitioners in Advertising, 2nd edition, 1985
Case Studies in Marketing Research
U Bradley; Van Nostrand Reinhold, 1982

ADVANCED MEDIA STUDIES

Introduction

This syllabus covers all aspects of the media function. It is assumed that before tackling the examination all candidates have a broad understanding of the basis of media. Advanced Media Studies moves on to areas of strategy rather than straightforward implementation. A good awareness of current developments in the media field is required together with an ability to present arguments in a lucid and convincing manner.

Aim

The aim of this module is to introduce students to media strategy. On completion of the module students will understand the role of media within overall marketing planning; relationship between media, agencies and client; media planning and the role of research.

Objectives

- To show the role of media planning within the overall marketing plan
- To show the sources of and use of
  - (a) research on media groups
  - (b) marketing data and
  - (c) media research
- To describe the media planning and control process
- To describe and analyse the media, agency and client relationship
- To describe the alternatives to mainstream media
- To show the 'influencers' in the media relation process.

Syllabus

- The role of media planning within the overall marketing plan
- Conversion of marketing requirements into a media brief
- Sources and use of marketing data (Nielsen, TCA, TGI, etc) for media selling and media planning
- How the media owner can influence media planning
- Inter-media comparisons
- The creative influence on media planning
- Relationship between media, agency and client
- Sources and use of media research data for media selling and media planning
- Influence upon media selection of type of product, method of distribution, campaign objectives, buying motive, influence upon the retail trade, timing, length of

advertising message, atmosphere, competition, size of appropriation
- Selecting the primary media group
- Selecting sub-groups
- Campaign weightings by product purchase, age/class, region, etc
- Media availability
- Computers in media
- The media plan
- Direct response advertising
- Media evaluation
- Alternatives to mainstream media. Sponsorship, sales promotion, exhibitions, public relations, etc.

Reading List

Essential
Spending Advertising Money
Simon Broadbent and Brian Jacobs; Business Books
Glossary of Advertising Terms, ISBA

Supplementary/Other
ADMAP (monthly)
Media World (monthly)
Media students are advised to be familiar with recent editions of all the Joint Industry Committee surveys and reports covering television, press and radio, and also to read the occasional papers issued by such organisations as the Screen Advertising Association, poster companies, etc.

Bibliography

Argyle, M, *Bodily Communication*, Methuen, 1976.

Bennis, W G, *Organisation Development: its Nature, Origins and Prospects*, Addison-Wesley, 1969.

Berne, E, *Games People Play*, Penguin, 1971.

Bernstein, D, *Corporate Image and Reality*, Holt, Rinehart and Winston, 1984.

Biddlecombe, P (Ed), *Goodwill – the Wasted Asset*, Business Books, 1971.

Boswell, J, *The Rise and Decline of Small Firms in Britain*, Allen & Unwin, 1972.

Bowman, P and Ellis, N, *Manual of Public Relations*, Heinemann, 1977.

Burke, W W, 'A comparison of management development and organisation development', *Management Science*, 1971.

Burns, T and Stalker, G M, *The Management of Innovation*, Tavistock, 1961.

Child, J, *Managerial and Organisational Factors Associated with Company Performance*, University of Aston Working Paper, Series No. 4, October 1973.

Child, J, *Organisation – a Guide to Problems and Practice*, Harper & Row, 1977.

Coulson-Thomas, C, *Public Relations is Your Business*, Business Books, 1981.

Coulson-Thomas, C, *Public Relations: A Practical Guide*, Macdonald and Evans, 1979.

de Bono, E, *The Use of Lateral Thinking*, Penguin, 1971.

185

Derriman, J, *Public Relations in Business Management*, University of London Press, 1964.

Drew, J, *Doing Business in the European Community*, Butterworth, 1979.

Fromm, E, 'Thoughts on bureaucracy', *Management Science*, 16, No. 12, August 1970.

Goffman, E, *Presentation of Self in Everyday Life*, Penguin, 1959.

Greenwood, W and Welsh, T (ed), *Essential Law for Journalists*, Butterworth, 1982.

Handy, C B, *Understanding Organisations*, Penguin, 1976.

Harrison, R, 'When power conflicts trigger team spirit', *European Business*, Spring 1972.

Hart, E P and Prais, S J, 'The analysis of business concentration', *Journal of the Royal Statistical Society*, Series A, Part 2 (1956), pp 150–81.

Haywood, R, *All About PR*, McGraw-Hill, 1984.

Hermann, C F, 'Some consequences of crisis which limit the viability of organisations', *Administrative Science Quaterly*, June 1963, pp 61–82

Hollis, *Press and Public Relations Annual*, 1986.

Howard, W (ed), *The Practice of Public Relations*, Heinemann, 1982.

Jefkins, F, *Planned Press and Public Relations*, Blackie, 1986.

Johns, E A, 'Where smallness pays', *Management Today*, July 1976.

Kahn, R L et al., *Organisational Stress*, Wiley, 1974.

Katz, D and Kahn, R L, *The Social Psychology of Organisations*, Wiley, 1966.

Kesey, K, *One Flew Over the Cuckoo's Nest*, Picador, 1976.

March, J G and Simon, H A, *Organisations*, Wiley, 1958.

Markham, V, *Planning the Corporate Reputation*, Allen & Unwin, 1972.

Mead, G H, *Mind, Self and Society*, University of Chicago Press, 1969.

Mendes, N, *This PR Consultancy Business*, Mendes, 1984.

Merrett, A J and Lehr, M E, *The Private Company Today: an Investigation into the Economic Position of the Unquoted Company in the United Kingdom*, Gower Press, 1971, p 25.

Moore, George S, *Managing Corporate Relations*, Gower Press, 1980.

Mueller, R K, *Career Conflict: Management Inelegant Dysfunction*, Arthur D Little, Lexington, D C Heath, 1978.

Newman, K, *Financial Marketing and Communications*, Holt, Reinhart and Winston, 1984.

Peters, M, *In Search of Excellence*, Harper & Row, 1984.

Pettigrew, A M, 'The influence process between specialists and executives', *Personnel Review*, Vol 3, No 1, Winter 1974.

Porter, M E, *Cases in Competitive Strategy*, Collier Macmillan, 1983.

Pugh, D S, 'Role activation conflict and a study of industrial inspections', *American Sociological Review*, Vol 31, No. 6, 1966, pp 836–42.

Pugh, D S and Hickson, D J, *Organisational Structure in its Context: the Aston Programme* I, Saxon House, Lexington Books, 1976.

Samuels, J M and Smythe, D J, 'Profits, variability of profits and firm size', *Economica*, May 1968, pp 127–38.

Ridgway, J, *Successful Media Relations: A Practitioner's Guide*, Gower, 1984.

Sartre, J-P, *The Reprieve*, Hamish Hamilton, 1947.

Schoeffler, S, Buzzell, R D and Heany, D F, 'Impact of strategic planning on profit performance', *Harvard Business Review*, March–April 1974, pp 137–45.

Schon, D A, *Beyond the Stable State*, Temple Smith, 1971.

Silver, P, 'Critical masses', *Accountancy Age*, March 1978.

Smith, G, *Local Government for Journalists*, LGC Communications, 1986.

Solomon, E, 'Return on investment – the relation of book yield to true yield', *Research and Accounting Measurement*, American Accounting Association, 1966.

St P Slatter, S, 'Strategic planning for public relations', *Long Range Planning*, Vol 13, June 1980.

Toffler, A, *Future Shock*, Bodley Head, 1970.

Tunstall, J, *The Media in Britain*, Constable, 1983.

Vickers, Sir G, *Value System and Social Processes*, Pelican, 1970.

Watts, R, *Public Relations for Top Management*, Croner, 1977.

Weber, M, *The Theory of Social and Economic Organisation*, The Free Press, Glencoe, Illinois, 1947.